A2 Geography

UNIT 5

AQA

Specification A

Module 5: Challenge and Change in the Human Environment

Philip Allan Updates
Market Place
Deddington
Oxfordshire
OX15 0SE

tel: 01869 338652
fax: 01869 337590
e-mail: sales@philipallan.co.uk
www.philipallan.co.uk

© Philip Allan Updates 2004
ISBN 0 86003 686 3

This Guide has been written specifically to support students preparing for the AQA Specification A A2 Geography Unit 5 examination. The content has been neither approved nor endorsed by AQA and remains the sole responsibility of the author.

Printed by Information Press, Eynsham, Oxford

Environmental information
The paper on which this title is printed is sourced from managed, sustainable forests.

Contents

Introduction

■ ■ ■

Content Guidance

■ ■ ■

Questions and Answers

Introduction

About this guide

This guide is for A2 Geography students following the AQA Specification A course. It aims to guide you through Unit 5, which examines the content of **Module 5: Challenge and Change in the Human Environment**.

This guide will clarify:
- the content of the module so that you know and understand what you have to learn
- the nature of the unit test
- the geographical skills and techniques you need to know
- the standards you need to reach to achieve a particular grade
- the examination techniques you will require to improve your performance and maximise your achievement

This Introduction describes the structure of A2 Geography and outlines the aims of Module 5. It then provides an explanation of some of the key command words used in examination papers. There is also advice concerning geographical skills, and learning and revision techniques.

The Content Guidance section summarises the essential information of Module 5. It is designed to make you aware of the material that has to be covered and learnt, and of the underlying synoptic links with other elements within this and other modules. The appreciation of these links is essential at A-level.

The Question and Answer section provides sample questions and candidate responses at C-grade and A-grade level. Each answer is followed by a detailed examiner's response. It is suggested that you read through the relevant topic area in the Content Guidance section before attempting a question from the Question and Answer section and only read the specimen answers after you have tackled the question yourself.

The essay in this unit is synoptic. It assesses your knowledge and understanding across a range of subject matter and expects you to make links between the different aspects of geography covered in this and other modules.

A2 Geography

Many of you will have taken the AS examination at the end of the first year of a 2 year course. You have decided to continue to study for another year to take A-level, which will be maintained at the traditional A-level standard. However, some of you may be taking AS at the same time as A2, at the end of a 1 or 2 year programme.

AS Geography covers three of the six modules that contribute to the full A-level qualification. These are set out below to remind you of what you have covered in the AS. In order to demonstrate synopticity in the essay, you should refer to work you have covered at AS as well as A2.

Remember that A-level cannot be taken without AS; it is not a qualification in its own right.

AS

Unit 1		Unit 2		Unit 3		
Core Concepts in Physical Geography	+	Core Concepts in Human Geography	+	Geographical Skills	=	AS Geography
35% of AS marks (17½% of A-level marks)		35% of AS marks (17½% of A-level marks)		30% of AS marks (15% of A-level marks)		

A-level (AS plus the following)

Unit 4		Unit 5		Fieldwork Investigation — Unit 6 Coursework or Unit 7		
Challenge and Change in the Natural Environment	+	Challenge and Change in the Human Environment	+	Written Alternative	=	A-level Geography
15% of marks		15% of marks		20% of marks		

The aims of Module 5

This module aims to help you:
- learn and apply knowledge and understanding of human processes and their interactions and outcomes over space and time
- understand the influence people have on these processes and the effects the processes have on people
- apply this knowledge and understanding at a variety of scales
- develop an understanding of the relationships between people and their environments, and of the opportunities, challenges and constraints that face people in different places and environments
- learn and apply geographical skills
- understand that geography is dynamic
- reflect the importance of other people's and your own values and attitudes to issues and questions
- acquire a deeper understanding of the connections between different aspects of geography
- develop a greater ability to synthesise geographical information

These aims are very broad and can be applied to any study of human geography. After the study of the module, you will be able to demonstrate your understanding of the specified areas of human geography. You will also be able to use the relevant geographical skills, interpret what they reveal and be aware of the values and conflicts that arise from the study of geography.

Assessment objectives

There are four ways in which these are assessed in this unit:
- AO1 — Knowledge (27%)
- AO2 — Critical understanding (33%)
- AO3 — Application of knowledge and critical understanding to unfamiliar contexts (27%)
- AO4 — Selection and use of skills and techniques, including communication, appropriate to geographical studies (13%)

Remember that every mark gained is in response to you demonstrating these assessment objectives in your answers. Making sure that your answers are relevant to the question is therefore essential.

Examination skills

Before looking at typical examination questions and responses in the Question and Answer section, we will examine the broader skills that are essential for success in the examination. These fall into two areas: the meaning of the command words, and making the most effective use of the examination paper.

The importance of command words

Command words are used by the examiners to tell you what to do in order to answer examination questions effectively. The words are set out below, in an approximate order of difficulty, with an explanation of what they mean. All of these may be familiar from AS, with the addition of 'evaluate' and 'discuss' which are considered to be higher-level command words and thus more appropriate to A2.

Command word(s)	Meaning
Describe...	State simply what is requested. Explanation or further comment is not required.
Name/State...	Identify briefly. One word may be adequate, but it may be better to use a sentence if in any doubt.
Distinguish between...	Define and state the differences between. Linking terms, such as 'whereas' or 'on the other hand', are essential.
Outline...	Describe, with a specific focus, the geographical element requested. For example, 'Outline the main features of...' has more of a focus than 'Describe the main features of...'

Outline the reasons for...	Give reasons for, with a specific focus, the geographical element required. The response will be briefer than a full explanation.
Account for/ Explain/Why...?	Give reasons for. The marks will be awarded for these reasons, rather than for description.
Give reason(s) for...	Some explanation must be offered.
Describe and explain...	Both elements, description and explanation, must be present for full marks. Ensure that examples of the mentioned theme are used in the response.
Compare...	What are the similarities between? Some element of contrast may be present.
Contrast...	What are the differences between? Two separate accounts will not meet the needs of this command; there must be a specific contrast or distinction between the elements.
Examine...	Give an overview of the elements which affect the theme, i.e. outline and explain.
Assess/To what extent...?	This requires an assessment of the importance of the factors involved in the response. This would be in an extended prose answer, rather than a short one.
Evaluate...	This is an alternative to 'To what extent', and has an emphasis on the *relative* importance of the factors/ themes involved. It is likely to need an essay response. A conclusion should be reached.
Discuss...	This requires a full coverage of the themes, again needing an essay response, with a reasoned conclusion. A variety of themes, strategies and results should be covered.

The unit test

Module 5 is assessed by Unit 5. You have 1 hour 30 minutes to answer this paper, which accounts for 15% of the A-level Geography qualification. The paper is divided into two sections: resource-based questions in Section A and essay questions in Section B.

Section A

In Section A, there are three stimulus–response questions, one from each of the three elements: (1) Population pressure and resource management, (2) Managing cities: challenges and issues, and (3) Recreation and tourism. You have to answer *two* questions from Section A.

Each question is marked out of 15, so there are 30 marks for the stimulus–response questions, out of 90 for the whole paper. You are advised to spend about 30 minutes on Section A. This advice is on the front of the examination paper, and means you have about 15 minutes per question, including a little time for the selection of the questions.

The spacing on the stimulus–response questions allows two lines per mark for your response, which is written in the question book. It is therefore useful to allocate your time accordingly. The highest number of marks is for the last part, so you should allow just under half the time on each question for this section — about 7 minutes.

Try to keep within the lines allocated, but if this proves to be impossible, use the lined pages at the end of the question booklet, making sure that you indicate what you have done and identify each response clearly.

Response levels

Parts (a) and (b) of each stimulus–response question are given 4 marks, generally by point marking, but part (c) (worth 7 marks) is marked according to Levels. There are criteria for reaching these Levels depending on the quality of the geographical content and the use of geographical and English language. This part of each question requires a fuller development of geographical understanding and language skills.

The Levels are as follows:
- **Level 1** responses are basic, with perhaps one or two points without examples, and a simplistic style of writing that is not focused on the requirements of the question. Specialist vocabulary is lacking.
- **Level 2** responses show a clear understanding of the topic, with better use of language, and have points with examples that recognise the potential complexity of the subject matter. There is appropriate use of specialist vocabulary.
- **Level 3** responses show detailed understanding, include several points with examples, and are written in a sophisticated and effective style. There is confident use of specialist vocabulary and a focus on the requirements of the question.

The command words are important, so make sure you remember to follow the instructions.

Section B

There are three essay questions in Section B, one from each of the three elements of the module. You have to answer one question from these three. They are marked out of 30 and the mark is doubled to give a mark out of 60, out of a total of the 90 marks available on the whole paper. The advice is to spend 60 minutes on this section, including planning time.

The questions are one-part essays, and advice to candidates about the need for synopticity appears above the essay titles. The essays are wide ranging in subject in order to allow candidates to develop synoptic themes using other elements of the specification. Fuller details can be found in the Question and Answer section of this guide.

Your answers are written in the question book. Several lined pages are supplied for this purpose. (If you do not have enough sheets, additional sheets can be requested; make sure that you attach these firmly to the question book.)

Response levels

Essays are marked by means of Levels, of which there are five in all, as follows:

- **Level 1** A very weak answer with little attempt to follow the theme. A low level of knowledge and understanding is shown, and the answer is inaccurate and poorly organised. Poor communication skills are shown, with many errors in spelling and grammar.
- **Level 2** A very mediocre answer, only occasionally relevant to the theme. Decidedly deficient in knowledge and understanding, with interrelationships lacking relevance and an increasingly descriptive response which may drift into another answer. Support is scanty and frequently inaccurate. Communication skills are basic, including many errors in spelling and grammar.
- **Level 3** A satisfactory answer at the upper end and mediocre at the lower end of the band. There is a reasonable grasp of knowledge, but understanding is suspect in places. The interconnections between elements of the specification are briefly mentioned. Support is not detailed, is occasionally inaccurate and is inconsistent. Communication skills are appropriate.
- **Level 4** A good answer, remaining relevant to the theme. Evaluation is implicit, with a confident range of knowledge, but with some omissions. There is reference to a range of subject matter from other elements of the specification (synoptic). Support is present but not always detailed. Communication skills are effective.
- **Level 5** A very good answer, consistently relevant to the theme. There is explicit evaluation and the command words are clearly followed, with the use of appropriate terminology and a confident range of knowledge from across the elements of the specification (synoptic). Support is consistent, accurate and detailed, and communication skills are detailed and sophisticated.

It is not possible to reach the top two mark bands without the synoptic links, which show the interrelationships between different elements of the specification, being identified clearly.

The examiners are looking for good organisation in these answers, so an introduction, a full development of the points to be made and a conclusion are very important. It is essential to have a plan; many candidates note points on the page before starting the essay. The suggested time for the essay question allows time for planning.

The introduction should set the scene. It does not have to be lengthy, but might include a definition of the terms used or the statement of the ideas to be developed.

The points to be developed usually appear as a series of paragraphs, one for each point, related to the theme of the question. The use of named and located cases is essential to ensure a good mark, as is the development of the interrelationships between the elements of the specification.

The conclusion in an essay summarises the main points made and refers to the question set. Remember to check the command words.

Geographical skills

As an integral part of your studies for this unit, you are required to develop and understand a variety of skills. The six types of geographical skill specified at AS are still relevant. These are:

- basic skills
- graphical skills
- cartographic skills
- ICT (information and communication technology) skills
- statistical skills
- investigative skills

A number of additional skills are specified for A2. The skills specified for AS are simply listed here. The A2 skills are described in more detail.

Basic skills

The levels of accuracy, sophistication and detail for the following basic skills are expected to be greater at A2:

- Base maps
- Sketch maps
- Atlas
- Photographs

Literacy
You need further to develop literacy skills during the A2 course. The assessment units require the ability to respond to both resource-based (structured) questions and essays.

Graphical skills

You should be familiar with the majority of these skills, but some will be new to you. You are expected to be able to interpret and construct the following:

- Line graphs — four types are specified
  - simple line graphs
  - comparative line graphs
  - compound line graphs
  - divergent line graphs
- Bar graphs — four types are specified
  - simple bar graphs
  - comparative bar graphs
  - compound (or divided) bar graphs
  - divergent bar graphs
- Scattergraphs — and the use of the best fit line
- Pie charts

- Triangular graphs
- Lorenz curves
- Kite and vector diagrams
- Pyramids
- Dispersion diagrams — these show the spread of data. They are usually in graph (point distribution) format, for example showing income per head. They show the mean and interquartile range.

Cartographic skills

- Ordnance Survey maps
- Choropleth (shading) and isoline maps
- Base maps — many of the graphical techniques listed above can be plotted on base maps.
- Maps with proportional symbols — squares, circles, semicircles or bars can be used to show values in a two-dimensional format. A greater range of values can be shown than on a linear representation, because the symbols increase in area rather than linearly. For instance, a value 100 times greater can be shown using a square with sides only 10 times greater (e.g. on a map showing numbers of tourists to countries in Europe).
- Maps showing movement — flow lines can be used on maps to show volumes of movement. The lines are proportional in width to the amount moved, for example on a map showing the number of people from different countries migrating to the UK. Trip and desire lines show the start and finish points of individual movements, for example the movements of shoppers to retail centres.

ICT (information and communication technology) skills

- Photographs
- Satellite images
- Databases
- Internet
- Video and television programmes
- Geographic information systems (GIS) — these are more flexible than standard databases, and link greater amounts of geographical data, including census data, local authority information, OS maps and satellite data.

Statistical skills

- Measures of central tendency — mean, mode and median
- Means of dispersion — interquartile range and standard deviation
- Correlation tests — at A2, in addition to **Spearman's rank correlation coefficient**, you need to be familiar with **Pearson's product moment correlation coefficient**. This is a more complicated, but more accurate, method of testing whether a relationship exists between sets of data. It measures the degree to

which a change in one variable is associated with changes in the other. It is used on data shown on a scattergraph and the outcome is a positive or negative relationship. The results are always within the range +1.0 (perfect positive correlation) to –1.0 (perfect negative correlation). It follows that a result closer to 0 indicates a weaker relationship (more like a clustered distribution). The minimum number of pairs of data is 6, although a minimum of 10 pairs ensures greater reliability. The test is used frequently, for example on the relationship between house prices and environmental quality index. At A2, you are expected to understand significance which, for Pearson, is calculated using the Student's t-test (see below).

- Comparative tests. The **chi-squared** test is used to compare the frequency distribution of two sets of variables. It does not measure correlation, but the association between the two sets of data. Observed frequencies (O) are compared with expected frequencies (E), and the probability of the differences occurring by chance is assessed. Data should always be in raw number form, with at least 20 values. A contingency table is constructed to compare E and O. The resulting individual cell values in this should show an expected frequency of 5 or more. If not, the categories (columns or rows) should be merged. The **Mann-Whitney test** is used when ranked data and data in the form of frequencies need to be compared, or where ranked samples of unequal size exist. The **Student's t-test** is used to measure the significance of a test and a given level of confidence for a particular sample size.

- Spatial distribution. **Nearest neighbour analysis** is used to measure the spatial distribution of data, in terms of the degree of clustering. At least 30 samples should be plotted on a map. The calculated result, which ranges from 0 to 2.14, can be shown by a linear scale, where 2.14 indicates perfect regularity, 1.0 indicates a random distribution, 0.23 linear clustering and 0 perfect clustering.

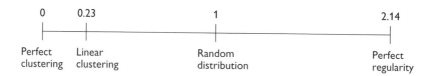

- The **index of dispersion** is frequently used with the **centre of gravity**. It measures the average distance of a feature from the 'centre of gravity' (the average of the coordinates of the feature). The degree of clustering is then demonstrated by the index of dispersion, drawn as a circle on a map, indicating a more clustered feature where the circle has a smaller radius.

- **Significance levels** indicate the probability of a result occurring by chance, and are usually assessed at a probability of 10%, 5% or 1%, the lower values being the more reliable. Statistical tables are available for this purpose. To use significance, a hypothesis (H_1) and a null hypothesis (H_0) have to be established. If the result is significant, H_0 is rejected and H_1 is accepted.

Investigative skills

- The identification of geographical questions and issues.
- The selection of relevant primary and secondary data and an assessment of their validity.
- The processing, presentation, analysis and interpretation of the evidence collected.
- The ability to draw conclusions and show an awareness of their validity.
- The awareness of risks when undertaking fieldwork.

Investigative skills are best developed by a programme of fieldwork undertaken in the AS and A2 years. Preparation for work in the field, the collection of data and their interpretation and evaluation are demonstrated clearly by writing up the fieldwork in the format suggested by the board. Your teachers will be able to advise you about this. At A2, the assessment of these skills takes place in Unit 6 or 7. Greater emphasis is also placed on the development of the stages of the enquiry, the drawing of conclusions and their validity.

Techniques for learning and revision

As in AS, there is no surplus of time available for teaching the subject content at A2. You must ensure that, from the start of your course, you establish good working practices to make the most of the time available:

- It is important not to fall behind with work during the year. New material will be taught each week, so, if you are unavoidably absent, for example because of illness, do make sure you make up the missed work as quickly as possible.
- You will probably have a steady stream of homework during the course. This is likely to take a variety of forms, ranging from working from the textbook or other sources, to practising examination questions.
- Read widely from a variety of sources, including your textbook, newspapers and magazines such as *Geography Review*. Television programmes are also relevant. The information you gather will enable you to develop a number of case studies for use in your examination answers.

The specification is divided up into modules, as we have already seen. Each module is divided into three elements and each of these is divided into sub-elements.

Module 5: Challenge and Change in the Human Environment is divided as follows:

Elements	Sub-elements
Population pressure and resource management	• Patterns, trends and concepts • Resource exploitation and management • The demographic response • The resource response: food surpluses in the MEDW • The resource response: food shortages in the LEDW

Elements	Sub-elements
Managing cities: challenges and issues	• Central area changes, causes and effects • Reversing the decline • Urban deprivation • Environmental issues
Recreation and tourism	• The resource base • 'Boom' in the MEDW • Expansion in the LEDW • Tourism and the environment • Tourism and development

Revision can be more easily structured by taking the sub-elements and focusing on them. Note that it is better to revise the sub-elements in the order in which they appear, or there is the risk that points will not make sense!

Some tips on revision

- Having selected a topic for revision, read and learn the material you have for this topic, for example notes, handouts, worksheets etc.
- Refer to your textbooks and to this publication. You might also find Raw, M. (2000) *AS/A-Level Geography Exam Revision Notes* (Philip Allan Updates) a useful guide.
- Learn the relevant case studies. You will need one or two for each element/sub-element and these should be at the specified scales.
- Practise sample questions, keeping to the appropriate timings. Use the questions in the last section of this guide for this purpose, taking care not to look at the sample answers and examiner's comments until you have attempted the questions. There are other specimen questions available, so consult your teacher/lecturer for advice.
- Apply your knowledge and understanding when practising so that your answers reflect the demands of the question.
- Allow yourself adequate time for revision. Little and often is usually better than concentrated pressure at the last minute.

Content
Guidance

There are three elements in the specification content for Module 5:

(1) Population pressure and resource management

(2) Managing cities: challenges and issues

(3) Recreation and tourism

In this section, the key concepts of each of these topics are explained, together with a breakdown of what you need to know and learn.

Points to note

- You are able to select two of the three elements for study, but this will reduce question choice. On the other hand, it will make the content much more manageable.
- Your teacher/lecturer will usually make the selection. You may need to be aware of the synoptic links with the element not studied.
- The number of references to case studies may seem daunting, but one or two case studies for each element is usually sufficient.
- All synoptic links in the specification are included in this section.

Population pressure and resource management

Patterns, trends and concepts

World population growth, including regional variations

In 2002, the population of the world reached 6.3 billion. The rate of increase is slowing after a rapid increase that started in western Europe after the industrial revolution. The most rapid growth took place in the twentieth century, initially in MEDCs, but also, during the second half of the century, in LEDCs.

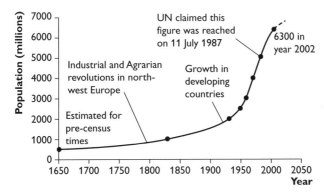

Reasons for these trends are given in the Unit 2 Guide in this series.

Within the global population growth figures, there is considerable regional variation, as shown in the table of percentage of world population by continent:

	Year			
	1800	**1900**	**2000**	**2050**
Europe	20.8	24.7	12.0	7.0
North America	0.7	5.0	5.1	4.4
Latin America	2.5	4.5	8.6	9.1
Africa	10.9	8.1	12.9	19.8
Asia	64.9	57.3	60.9	59.2
Oceania	0.2	0.4	0.5	0.5

Thus, from 2000 onwards, according to UN predictions, 100% of world population growth will occur in the LEDCs of Latin America, Africa and Asia, with the fastest rate of growth in Africa. The MEDCs' share of world population will therefore fall, even though their populations will be relatively stable.

You need to:
- know the growth trends of the world population, past, present and future
- be familiar with the regional variations, past, present and future
- be aware of the variations between the LEDW and the MEDW on a global scale

Underpopulation, overpopulation and optimum population

The concepts of underpopulation, overpopulation and optimum population underpin the study of population and resource relationships. These concepts are relative, and depend mainly on population and resource availability and the level of technology. The balance can be expressed as:

$$\text{standard of living} = \frac{\text{natural resources (e.g. minerals, soils, energy)} \times \text{technology}}{\text{population}}$$

The relationships are dynamic; each component can change over time.

Underpopulation

Underpopulation is the situation in which an increase in the population of an area would improve the population–resource ratio and raise standards of living. Alternatively, underpopulation can be expressed as 'too few people to exploit the available resources to the maximum potential'.

Canada is a possible example of underpopulation. Underpopulated areas export food and minerals, have high per capita incomes and standards of living, make use of advanced technology and allow immigration. An increase in population would permit raised standards of living by increasing output and exploitation of resources.

Overpopulation

Overpopulation is a situation in which a reduction in the population of an area would improve the population–resource ratio and raise standards of living. Alternatively, overpopulation can be expressed as 'too many people for the resources to be able to support the population to the maximum potential'.

Bangladesh is a possible example of overpopulation. Overpopulated areas suffer from droughts and/or flooding, which lead to famine because recurrent natural and man-made disasters prevent the resources being used to support the increasing population. Such areas have low per capita incomes, poor living conditions and are characterised by emigration.

Optimum population

The optimum population is the number of people in an area that can be sustained by the existing resources and technology at the highest standard of living. Population and resource exploitation are in balance.

Although the concept is relatively easy to define, it is difficult to identify an optimum population. This is because population is rarely stable and the resource base varies as old resources are exhausted and new ones are utilised. In addition, the level of technology varies and affects the use of the resources and their availability. Constant economic change means that the optimum is rarely achieved and retained for any length of time. Therefore, the population–resource balance is in a state of constant flux. However, the economies of many countries (mainly MEDCs) are considered to be close to the optimum.

Points to note
- Sustainability is the use of resources to meet current demand without compromising the ability of future generations to meet their own needs. There is clearly a link between sustainability and the concepts outlined here.
- Remember that the ability of an area to support its population is not necessarily related to population density. The Brazilian rainforest area has a low population density (5 per km^2) but this may be optimum for the level of resources. The Netherlands has a high population density, but is not overpopulated.

You need to:
- understand the concepts of underpopulation, overpopulation and optimum population
- understand that the relationships between population, resources and technology vary and influence the standard of living in an area
- understand the link between these concepts and that of sustainability

Theories of population–resource relationships

Malthus's theory
Thomas Malthus published his work in 1798. The two basic principles are that population grows at a geometric (exponential) rate and food supply increases at an arithmetic rate:
- population growth: $1 \rightarrow 2 \rightarrow 4 \rightarrow 8 \rightarrow 16 \rightarrow 32$
- food supply: $1 \rightarrow 2 \rightarrow 3 \rightarrow 4 \rightarrow 5 \rightarrow 6$

Thus, food supply will not be able to keep up with population growth and a population ceiling will be reached.

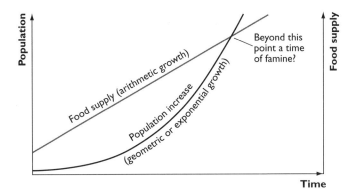

Malthus also suggested that positive checks (increasing mortality rates because of war, pestilence, famine or disease) and preventative checks (reducing fertility rates by postponing marriage as the economic circumstances deteriorated) would also limit population at or around this ceiling.

The concept of **carrying capacity** follows. This is the population that can be supported by the local environment. There are two models (S-curve and J-curve) that demonstrate change as the exponentially growing population approaches the ceiling. The S-curve is produced by the population growth tapering off as the ceiling is approached and levels out at the ceiling. The J-curve is produced when a population overshoots the ceiling, resulting in a sudden check that causes the population to fall rapidly. The population recovers and then oscillates above and below the ceiling before levelling out at the ceiling.

Boserup's studies

Boserup's studies came much later (1965). She takes a more optimistic view of the population–resource relationship, which can be summarised as 'necessity is the mother of invention'. Her studies indicated that, in a pre-industrial society, an increase in population stimulates agricultural output, i.e. the farming system responds to produce more food to meet the new demands, which in turn means that a higher population could be supported.

Neo-Malthusian views

Some recent studies have been neo-Malthusian in outlook, i.e. they are pessimistic about future population–resource ratios. One such was the Club of Rome Report (1972), *The Limits to Growth*. Five parameters were studied: population growth, natural resources, food supply, industrial output and pollution.

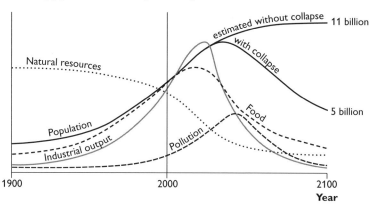

There are three main conclusions:
- First — within a time span of less than 100 years, with no major change in the physical, economic or social relationships governing development, society will run out of the non-renewable resources on which the industrial base depends. When the resources have been depleted, a precipitous collapse of the economic system will result, leading to massive unemployment, decreased food production, and a decline in population as the death rate soars. The characteristic behaviour of the system is overshoot and collapse.
- Second — piecemeal approaches to solving the individual problems will not be

successful. The removal of one limit (such as increasing resources) merely causes the system to bump subsequently into another one (such as increased pollution), usually with more dire consequences.

- Third — overshoot and collapse can be avoided only by an immediate limit on population and pollution. There are only two possible outcomes: the termination of growth by self-restraint and conscious policy (an approach that avoids the collapse) or the termination of growth by a collision with the natural limits.

Other recent theories (e.g. Khan, 1976) are more optimistic. They take the view that, as population, technology and resources adapt, there will be gradual adjustment and global stability will be reached by 2150, a similar pattern to that predicted by the S curve.

Case study

The case study of Sahelian Africa exemplifies the theories.

The Sahel is an area between the northern margins of the savanna grasslands and the southern edge of the Sahara, running in a belt from the Horn of Africa in the east to Mali in the west. The main countries are Ethiopia, Somalia, Sudan, Chad and Niger. This is a marginal area with regard to agriculture. The rains are extremely variable and total precipitation is low, as this area is at the northernmost margin of the rain belt that provides precipitation to the savanna. Arable farming is dependent on the rains; nomadic herders migrate to find water for their livestock. The natural vegetation is thorn scrub, with coarse grasses. Thus the resource base is limited and the carrying capacity is low. In recent years, the population has been increasing and at the same time there have been several years of drought, reducing the output from agriculture. In addition, the easternmost states have experienced war. This has further disrupted agriculture and lowered output. The ceiling in this area has been reached and the consequent famine has resulted in large numbers of people starving.

At present, this example is essentially Malthusian. However, many people consider that, given the availability of water when the rains occur and a period of political stability, this area will be able to support the population — an essentially optimistic view, as held by Boserup.

You need to:

- know that there are both pessimistic and optimistic theories of population–resource relationships
- know the theories of Malthus, Boserup and the Club of Rome
- be able to apply the theories to examples such as the Sahel
- understand the link between these concepts and that of sustainability

Synoptic links

- Unit 2, element 1
- Unit 4, element 2

Resource exploitation and management

Resources: definitions

Resources are defined as items that can be used by people. A broad classification is set out below:

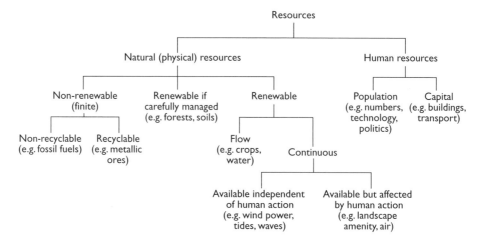

Reserves are known resources exploitable under current economic and technological conditions. **Stocks** are all available reserves, whether exploitable or not.

Renewable resources are those that can be reused repeatedly (infinite). Renewable sources of energy include hydroelectricity, wind, solar, tidal, wave, geothermal, nuclear and biomass. Other renewable resources, if conserved, are timber/forests, soil, crops, fish and water.

Non-renewable resources are those that can be exhausted (finite). Non-renewable sources of energy are coal, oil, natural gas, lignite and peat. Other non-renewable resources are minerals and, if not conserved, timber/forests, soil, crops, fish and water.

You need to:
- be able to classify resources
- be able to define components of the classification, including stocks, reserves, renewable and non-renewable

The life cycle of a resource

The overall life cycle of a non-renewable resource involves the following stages:
- discovery and early development
- initial rapid growth
- slower growth and maturity
- decline
- depletion

Generally, the life cycle starts with discovery, low initial production and slow growth followed by rapidly increasing production, then moderately increasing production to a maximum. Finally, production of the resource enters a period of decline until the resource is economically exhausted.

You need to:
- know the life cycle of a resource

Exploitation and management of resources

One renewable and *one* non-renewable resource must be studied at a global scale. The renewable resource must be either timber or water; the non-renewable resource must be chosen from iron ore, copper, coal or oil. The themes to be studied are:
- the environmental impact of resource exploitation and management
- resource exploitation and management in the context of sustainable development

These two themes are implicitly linked. The environmental impact and management of the resource exploitation are directly linked to the sustainability of the resource. Sustainability means using resources to meet current demand, without compromising the ability of future generations to meet their own needs.

A study of changing energy resource production and consumption, both at a global scale and in the UK, is relevant here. Information is readily available to meet the requirement for a non-renewable resource. You have already studied rainforests in Unit 1 and you could develop these for A2 to meet the requirement for a renewable resource. However, other examples are also pertinent.

You need to:
- be familiar with the environmental impact of resource exploitation and management in the context of sustainable development of one renewable and one non-renewable resource
- be able to apply the concept of sustainability to the selected resources

Synoptic links
- Unit 1, elements 1 and 3
- Unit 2, element 3
- Unit 4, elements 2 and 3

The demographic response

The population–resource balance and rapid population growth

There is increasing concern about the effects of rapid population growth on the population–resource balance. This has led to the identification of a number of indicators to measure this balance that use development and welfare criteria. These indicators are used to make comparisons between countries and areas.

Demographic indicators

(Definitions are only included if they are not given elsewhere in the unit guides.)

Indicator	Definition/Use	Evaluation
Crude birth rate per thousand population	High rates tend to indicate a low level of economic development	By themselves, these four indicators provide only limited information

They are more valid when considered with other indicators, including those from the economic and social criteria tables below

Data reliability is variable; in general, data from countries with higher levels of economic development are more reliable

The indicators are also set at a national level; they are averages that may mask significant internal spatial variations |
Crude death rate per thousand population	High rates tend to indicate a low level of economic development	
Fertility rate per thousand women aged 15–49	High rates tend to indicate a low level of economic development	
Infant mortality rate per thousand live births	High rates tend to indicate a low level of economic development	
Population structure	The balance between the age groups reflects the level of economic development

A large proportion of under 16s tends to indicate a lower level

A large proportion of over 65s tends to indicate a higher level | These two indicators are important in their own right

When the economic consequences of the proportion of population in the various age groups are considered, they indicate the relative level of economic development in the country |
| Dependency ratio | The ratio between the numbers economically active (16–65) and economically inactive (under 16 and over 65)

The higher the proportion of economically inactive, the more people there are who are economically dependent on those in work | |
| Life expectancy in years | The greater the life expectancy, the higher the level of economic development | This is summative of the demographic indicators |

Economic indicators

(Definitions are only included if they are not given elsewhere in the unit guides.)

Indicator	Definition/use	Evaluation
Gross domestic product (GDP)	The sum of the value of all goods and services produced in a country, divided by its population It measures the domestic output per head of population in US dollars	These four indicators may be used to show the relative wealth of a country GDP is easier to measure than GNP GDP and GNP are good indicators, being measured in a single currency, despite the effects of currency fluctuations
Gross national product (GNP)	Net trade and currency movements are added to GDP; the total is divided by the population This is a broader measure of output per head than GDP	Economic data are more reliable when transactions are measured in market economies; when trade is informal (e.g. in cash or by barter), data are less reliable These indicators are crude averages and mask internal socioeconomic and spatial variations
Energy consumption per capita	The higher the energy use, the greater the level of economic development	
Material goods per capita or household	Indicators include telephones, cars, television sets and certain other electrical goods	
Purchasing power	The value of local income in comparison with the amount it can buy, e.g. the cost of a Big Mac in different countries, relative to wages More recent studies have used more complex data	An alternative to income per head (GDP or GNP) It accommodates currency fluctuations and shows the relative prices for different types of good It is a more accurate and reliable indicator
Employment structure	The proportion of workers employed in the primary, secondary and tertiary sectors of the economy changes with economic development It moves from a large proportion in primary, via secondary, to a large proportion in tertiary	Reflects changes in the level of economic development Poorer countries have a large primary sector; richer countries have declining primary and secondary sectors and an expanding tertiary sector

Social indicators

(Definitions are only included if they are not given elsewhere in the unit guides.)

Indicator	Definition/use	Evaluation
Disease	Incidence of disease indicates the relative wealth of the area Some diseases are related to malnutrition (e.g. rickets, beri-beri, and kwashiorkor) and to poor hygiene (e.g. cholera); others are related to diet/lifestyle (e.g. cancers, heart disease, obesity), especially in more developed countries	The type of disease is indicative of the standard of living in an area All social indicators are of more use when applied with economic and demographic indicators
Health care, e.g. doctors per capita, hospital beds per capita	The ratio of health professionals to the population in an area The lower the ratio, the greater is the investment in health care	Frequently used as a measure of the level of development Data may not be collected reliably It is an average figure, masking internal variations
Education	The number or proportion of children in primary and/or secondary education indicates the wealth of a country	A crude measure, with some validity
Literacy rate	The percentage of the population able to read	A frequently used indicator of economic development, with fair validity

Composite quality-of-life indicators

The most effective indicators are indices, calculated by combining a variety of indicators.

The **physical quality-of-life index (PQLI)** is the average of literacy, life expectancy and infant mortality. When introduced, it was an improvement on individual indicators, but it was replaced by the **human development index (HDI)**, which incorporates life expectancy, education and income and is scored between 0 and 1. The data used are more complex. For example, education incorporates the adult literacy rate and the average number of years at school; income refers to the income per capita converted to purchasing parity in US dollars. Developed countries have a score of 0.9 and the poorest countries a score of less than 0.25.

Evaluation

- The link between the HDI and the GDP is clear, because the indicators are dependent on a country's wealth.
- HDI is considered to be a more effective index because of the range of indicators included in its calculation.
- HDI over-values economic indicators.

- The range of values permits the identification of the relative wealth of countries.
- The identification of a development continuum is possible when the level of development of MEDCs and LEDCs is continuous and without steps when plotted on a graph.

You need to:
- know that the indicators used to measure development are demographic, economic and social
- understand that each indicator has limited validity
- be aware that composite indices such as PQLI and HDI are more effective measures of development
- understand that a continuum of levels of economic development, rather than one with steps and gaps, can be identified

Synoptic links
- Unit 2, element 1

Population–resource imbalances: population policies

A number of responses to population–resource imbalances are possible. These include policies to control population growth, increase population and/or increase resources. You are required to study two cases of population control (**anti-natalist**) policies and one case of a population increase (**pro-natalist**) policy.

The anti-natalist case of China is well documented. The one-child policy was introduced in 1979 and was particularly effective in towns and cities. The original inflexible policy has been modified, but the overall effect has been to reduce both the birth rate and the size of the average family. Therefore, the rate of population growth has slowed, but not to the intended level, because the population exceeded 1.2 billion before the year 2000.

Other countries with anti-natalist policies are India and Mauritius, both of which are frequently studied.

There are fewer cases of pro-natalist policies. One frequently studied is France, which established policies to increase its population after the losses in the First World War (1914–18). There were various incentives for women to have children, including financial support, medals and free holidays for the children. In recent years, the population has increased. However, this has also been the result of immigration from former colonies and the higher birth rates of many of these groups.

You need to:
- know the responses to population–resource imbalance
- know two cases of anti-natalist policies
- know one case of a pro-natalist policy

Population–resource imbalances: migration controls and transmigration

Many countries, particularly in the MEDW, have **immigration controls**. These controls are to prevent large numbers of people entering the country. Many countries permit selective immigration, taking those who are considered to be essential workers. The UK has a policy that restricts the numbers of unskilled and low-skilled migrants, but permits much freer movement of those with a high level of skills and/or wealth. The USA has controls on its southern frontiers to restrict the number of migrants from Mexico, the Caribbean and Central and South America. This is only partially successful and large numbers of migrants enter the country each year. The economies of California and the southern states depend on these 'illegals' and from time to time an amnesty is granted. This migration has caused the Hispanic population of the USA to increase rapidly and therefore to gain much political power.

Transmigration is used in a small number of cases by governments to try to balance the distribution of population. The migration can be voluntary, based on incentives, as in Brazil. In this case, the opening of the Amazonian rainforest areas to farmers, with land provided for those who migrate, has continued for over 30 years. The construction of Brasilia as the capital provided a great impetus for this migration.

In the case of Indonesia, transmigration was forced. The population of Java, Bali and Madura was increasing. The transmigration policy was to balance demographic and economic development, alleviate poverty by providing land and to exploit the potential of the outer, less densely populated islands (Sumatra, Irian Jaya, Kalimantan, Aceh and East Timor). Between 1949 and 1974, 640 000 people were resettled; between 1975 and 2000 a further 3.5 million were moved.

You need to:
- understand the role of migration controls on population–resource imbalance
- understand the role of transmigration policies on population–resource imbalance

Issues surrounding the responses to population–resource imbalances

Population and migration policies have consequences. Some of these are set out below and applied to the Chinese anti-natalist and Indonesian transmigration policies.

Consequence	Chinese anti-natalist policy	Indonesian transmigration policy
Social	<ul><li>Smaller families</li><li>Preponderance of male children</li><li>Fewer marriages as children grow up</li><li>Spoilt, only children</li><li>Coercion and brutality used to achieve aims</li></ul>	<ul><li>Forced movement of families</li><li>Break-up of extended family groups</li><li>Friction with indigenous peoples</li><li>Insurrection (migrants targeted by local people)</li></ul>

Consequence	Chinese anti-natalist policy	Indonesian transmigration policy
Economic	• Better population–resource ratio • Education and jobs available • Smaller labour force	• More land used for farming • High costs of programme led to its suspension after an economic crisis in 1997 • Has redistributed poverty • No decline in population density in core areas
Political	• Policy unpopular • The policy was modified later in rural areas	• Transmigration used to try to suppress and control the indigenous population (East Timor, Aceh, Irian Jaya) • Two changes of president/ government after 1997
Cultural	• Change in family values • Female infanticide increased	• Friction between two culturally distinct peoples
Environmental	• Less pressure on resources	• Destruction of large areas of rainforest

You need to:
- understand that all policies in response to population–resource imbalance have consequences
- know that these can be social, economic, political, cultural and environmental
- explore your own attitudes and values to these issues

Synoptic links
- Unit 1, element 3
- Unit 2, element 3

The resource response: food surpluses in the MEDW

Developed world surpluses

One of the major features of farming in the developed world is the production of food surpluses. These have arisen for a number of reasons, including economies of scale, organisational change, intensification of agriculture and government support.

Although surpluses are a feature of many developed countries, the example to be studied is the application of the Common Agricultural Policy (CAP) in the EU. The policy was established in order to:
- increase agricultural productivity and improve self-sufficiency
- maintain jobs on the land, preferably on family farms
- improve the standard of living of farmers and farmworkers

- stabilise markets
- keep consumer food prices stable and reasonable

Most of these objectives have been achieved. By a combination of market forces and financial incentives, farming has become more efficient. This has been achieved through a combination of a number of changes, including:
- increased use of machinery
- consolidation of farms into larger units and removal of hedgerows to enlarge fields
- greater use of hybrid seeds and similar animal breeding techniques
- use of fertilisers, herbicides and pesticides
- greater capital investment

The CAP has provided much of the financial support for these changes in the form of guaranteed prices for produce, grants for specifics such as hedgerow removal, and also intervention price support, whereby farmers' produce is bought at a guaranteed intervention price if there is no demand for it.

This led to increased yields of crops and animal output, in particular cereals, milk, wine, butter and beef, frequently referred to as 'mountains' or 'lakes', as appropriate.

Case study on a regional scale

Southern Italy has been the recipient of financial support since the 1950s, initially under the Casa per il Mezzogiorno and, more recently, as a Section 1 region of the EU. Traditionally, farming has had low-capital and high-labour inputs. Summers are hot and dry, winters mild and wet. Outputs per hectare are usually low, being strongly affected by local physical conditions. Citrus fruits, vines, olives and wheat are the main products; sheep and goats are the main livestock. Consolidation of farms has taken place, with older farmers being pensioned off to facilitate this. Cooperatives have been established to improve the marketing of produce. However, change has been slow because of the distance from the main European markets.

Case study on a small scale

Pressures on the urban fringe can be seen around large cities in the UK. Horticulture has been developed to feed the large urban population. This includes the production of salad vegetables, soft fruits and orchard crops. The high price of land and urban expansion has resulted in a decline in the production of these crops around, for example, London and their cultivation in other areas of the UK and Europe (e.g. Spain, France, Italy and Turkey) that are more climatically favourable to their growth. Many former horticultural farms have become pick-your-own (PYO) farms, whereby the products are the same but the purchaser provides the labour for harvest.

You need to:

- understand the reasons for the production of farm surpluses in the MEDW
- be familiar with the effects of the CAP on farming in the EU
- know a regional case study, such as southern Italy
- know a small-scale case study, such as the urban fringe

The economic, social and environmental consequences of farm surpluses

As the size of the surpluses increased, it became clear that there were a number of negative consequences, caused mainly by capital-intensive farming.

Economically, the surpluses were using a sizeable proportion of the EU's annual budget in the costs of storage, export, intervention subsidies and disposal. Consumer prices were higher to meet the costs of the CAP. CAP spending was concentrated on the most efficient farms and marginal farms did not gain the same levels of support. The economic impact on LEDCs as the subsidised food was allowed into home markets destroyed the market for locally produced food.

The changes to agriculture caused social change. As farms were consolidated, older farmers retired, family farms were sold off or abandoned, particularly if they were very small and in marginal areas. There was a movement from rural to urban areas. Commuters took over houses near large cities; many rural areas became areas of second homes.

Environmentally, hedgerow removal resulted in soil erosion because the larger fields were exposed to greater wind speeds and overland flow. Habitats for birds, mammals and insects were lost. Erosion increased as a result of monoculture, and soils were degraded further by the application of inorganic fertilisers. In addition, the nitrates in these fertilisers contaminated groundwater supplies.

In response to concerns arising from the points above, the CAP was modified and the policy moved towards one of sustainable farming, though progress has been variable. Set-aside has been operating for a number of years. This involves farmers being paid *not* to grow crops on their land in an attempt to reduce surpluses. Farmers have responded by taking marginal land out of cultivation, so the decrease in output has not been as great as expected.

Organic farming has become more important as a number of farmers have moved to this less intensive method of production. Although organic crops are more expensive, in the aftermath of foot-and-mouth disease, swine fever, BSE and other health concerns, consumers are prepared to pay the premium.

In recent years, the costs of generating agricultural produce have increased and prices have fallen. Many farmers, particularly in the UK, have gone out of business. Others have diversified away from agricultural production into allied activities such as woodland and meadow planting, for which there is financial support, and tourism/holiday homes, for which there is not.

It is worth noting that not all farming activities gain subsidies. For example, pig and poultry farming, horticulture and orchard crops depend on free-market prices and have faced increasing competition from cheaper overseas producers, with the result that UK production has declined.

In more recent years, **genetically modified (GM)** crops have been a source of either great hope or concern. Crops can be modified in a number of ways, for example to be resistant to certain pests, viruses and diseases so that the use of chemicals can be targeted, with subsequent cost savings. In addition, allergenicity can be reduced and nutritional content improved. The increase in yields could, it is claimed, help to supply areas of the world that are unable to feed their populations. The fear of cross-pollination with non-GM crops is frequently raised and the consequences of such an event have not been tested. It is feared that GM crop cross-pollination will result in the disappearance of all organic crops. 99% of GM crops, in particular soya beans, maize and cotton, are currently grown in the USA, Canada, China and Argentina. At the time of writing, in the EU no GM crop has been approved for growth or sale since 1998, despite great pressure to do so. Some LEDCs have rejected food aid that includes GM maize.

You need to:

- understand that farming surpluses in the MEDW have economic, social and environmental consequences
- know that responses include set-aside, organic farming and diversification
- know that GM crops have positive and negative attributes
- explore your values and attitudes and those of others to organic farming and GM crops
- be able to apply the concept of sustainability to these issues

Synoptic links

- Unit 1, element 3
- Unit 2, element 3

The resource response: food shortages in the LEDW

Shortages of food in the LEDW: traditional farming systems

The greatest areas of food shortage are considered by many to be in Africa. Here farming, whether arable or pastoral, was traditionally extensive. Low yields were achieved from low inputs. As population pressure has risen, there has been some adaptation, but a combination of natural hazards and over-farming has lowered yields in recent years. This is the only area of the world where this has occurred.

The Sahel is frequently quoted in this context. This area of Africa lies to the north of the savanna belt. It has a low, variable rainfall, which occurs in summer, and there is a long period of drought (9 months or so). The natural vegetation is semi-desert scrub and tussock grass. Thus, farming is marginal, being in the form of livestock grazing and, where possible, growing millet as the main cereal crop. Overgrazing by livestock has been a serious problem and the removal of trees for firewood has resulted in serious deforestation. Soil erosion has followed, causing population pressure (the population has been increasing at over 2% per annum). During the 1980s, it was thought that the climate of the Sahel was changing because the rains failed for several years. At the same time, there was a period of political instability in many of the countries in this area and, as a result of wars, agriculture was disrupted and planted crops remained unharvested. Famine ensued and much international food aid was needed to avert starvation of large numbers of people. The causes of this situation were, therefore, both natural and human.

You need to:
- understand the reasons for shortages of food in the LEDW
- be aware that these reasons are the result of both natural (physical) and human influences

Modernisation of agriculture

In other parts of the world, there has been a more positive response. Despite frequent natural hazards such as flooding, hurricanes and droughts, and human influences such as political instability, food output has kept up with population increase to a greater extent, although in recent years population growth has slowed in many countries in the LEDW.

The agricultural reasons for this resource balance are varied. In many parts of the world, including some parts of Africa, Brazil, the Punjab and the Philippines, the increases in output are the result of partial modernisation. The most important changes include the green revolution, the introduction of cash crops, the role of transnational companies and the expansion of agricultural frontiers.

The green revolution involved the use of hybrid plants, with maize (in Mexico) and rice (in the Philippines) the first crops planted. These hybrids yielded greater harvests of much needed foodstuffs. However, they required inputs of fertilisers and capital, so only the better-off farmers were able to benefit fully. Many poorer farmers left the land and moved to the cities. In the Punjab, the increased use of irrigation depleted water supplies and caused salinisation of the groundwater. Modernisation in Bangladesh has been hindered by regular coastal and fluvial flooding, causing disruption to farming and loss of life. Overall, food supply in the LEDW has increased as a result of the green revolution.

The increase in the production of cash crops has been variable and is frequently linked to the role of transnational companies. Kenya has a thriving cash-crop economy, supplying fresh vegetables to UK supermarkets. Coffee, cotton and tea are also important cash crops here. Until the recent disruption to farming as a result of political instability, Zimbabwe also supplied the UK.

Agricultural frontiers expanded in Brazil and Indonesia, where transmigration occurred. Land was allocated to new farmers with variable success. Initial results were encouraging, but fertility fell in subsequent years.

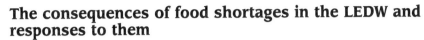

The consequences of food shortages in the LEDW and responses to them

Despite the efforts made to work with traditional farming systems and attempts at modernisation using a variety of techniques and policies, intermittent famine and malnutrition are frequent occurrences, for example in the Sahel. The ability of a country to respond depends to a great extent on its level of economic development. The LEDW has countries at various levels of development; thus responses are variable.

As measured by the GDP, the lowest levels of development are in Africa. Therefore, it is not surprising that many African countries have the greatest food shortages. Countries with higher levels of development, such as Indonesia and Brazil, are better placed to feed the population. It is clear that the use of appropriate technology is necessary. This is to ensure that both the hi-tech approaches of the MEDW and local knowledge of potential improvements in the LEDW can be effective. This would achieve the level of essential sustainability if the population–resource balance were not to deteriorate.

The link between the MEDW and the LEDW is an essential element of the concept of global interdependence. The relationship is demonstrated by trade patterns and by the provision of aid. The World Trade Organization (WTO) is important in maintaining the links, though the relationship itself tends to be dominated by the MEDW. Despite the oft-stated intention of the MEDW to increase world trade and assist the LEDW in raising levels of economic development, little is done if MEDW interests are threatened. This was apparent in the Cancún round of WTO talks in 2003. In fact, aid levels are tending to decrease, unless they are in the form of tied aid or the political and cultural views of the donor nations are imposed on the receiving countries.

You need to:
- know the consequences of food shortages in the LEDW
- understand that the effective management of food shortages is dependent on the level of economic development of the country
- be aware that the need to ensure appropriate technology and sustainability is an important element in strategies to reduce food shortages
- understand that global interdependence means that the LEDW and the MEDW are dependent on each other for economic development and sustainability
- explore your attitudes and those of others to these themes

Synoptic links
- Unit 1, elements 2 and 3
- Unit 2, elements 1 and 3
- Unit 5, element 3

Managing cities: challenges and issues

Central area changes: causes and effects

The decline of central area business

Many central area functions have declined in importance in recent years. This decentralisation is a result of the diseconomies of scale associated with a CBD location in comparison with other locations in the urban area. The main functions involved are certain types of retailing and offices (see below).

The main causes include:
- the high cost of land and rentals in the CBD
- increasing levels of congestion (whatever the form of transport) and the consequent costs
- the need to pay higher wages and salaries
- the costs and time involved in travelling to and from work
- the relative advantages of other sites
- the age or obsolescence of the buildings

You need to:
- know the reasons for the decline of central area business

The effects of central area decline

The main retailing functions to decentralise are food, DIY and electrical goods. These retail functions are now associated with superstores, usually situated in the suburbs or urban fringes. Apart from the high cost of land, it is unusual for large sites to become available in the central areas of cities. The parking requirements of customers cannot be met because of the lack of available land and the congestion that would result.

The flight to the fringe by retailing has been replicated to an extent by some types of office, giving rise to the 'dead heart' concept, i.e. the decline of the centre of cities as the functions move out. If the decline is concentrated, a zone of discard may be identified. This includes empty and, in some cases, derelict buildings as well as low-grade CBD functions. The intensity of land use also declines. This effect can also be seen where land use is about to, or is expected to, change, for example if a high-rise office block is to be constructed on an area of existing land.

In some cities, decentralisation and the availability of vacant sites have created space for beneficial changes to the central area. In particular, leisure and tourist facilities have been established and expanded. For example, in London, the riverside downstream from Tower Bridge has been converted into tourist, restaurant and retail facilities. This is the case both north (St Catherine's Dock) and south (Butler's Wharf) of the River Thames. In other cases, specialised shopping areas have been developed. Similar examples are to be found in cities and towns in your local area.

You need to:

- know the effects of central area decline on retailing and other functions
- understand the 'dead heart' concept
- be familiar with other changes, including the development of specialised shopping areas and the expansion of leisure facilities
- know a small-scale case study to exemplify the above

Synoptic links

- Unit 2, elements 2 and 3

Reversing the decline

New developments

Decentralisation has provided new opportunities in the central areas of cities. These include large-scale retail development, office expansion, the growth of tourist facilities, the improvement of central areas with regard to conservation, pedestrianisation, marinas and gentrified areas. Most cities in the UK have some or all of these features.

London has new retail developments in suburban centres, such as Brent Cross, the Whitgift Centre in Croydon and the Glades in Bromley. The first is a new, purpose-built centre; the others are additions to existing shopping centres. In central London, smaller developments have taken place within existing retail areas, for example, the Trocadero in Oxford Street and the redevelopment of part of Covent Garden.

Office development has occurred in suburban centres, particularly Croydon. The spectacular new office block concentration at Canary Wharf is a testament to the viability of London as a financial centre as businesses have moved out of the City. International organisations have played a major role in these trends. Canary Wharf contains the international headquarters of companies such as HSBC, whose tower block replaced 17 other offices in London. There are now six further tower blocks built around the Canary Wharf tower itself. This office concentration has attracted a number of high-quality retailers in Jubilee Square to meet the needs of the thousands of office workers. These include Waitrose/John Lewis, Marks and Spencer, 31 retailers of designer brands of clothing and a variety of restaurants and food outlets. In Canary Wharf, there are 141 retail facilities.

Tourist facilities and areas have been enhanced. This can be seen in central London, where tourism is an essential part of the economy of the West End, and along the River Thames, especially downstream from Tower Bridge. These changes have often gone hand-in-hand with pedestrianisation schemes, such as Trafalgar Square and Leicester Square in central London and the development of walkways along the River Thames. Hotels have been built as part of these changes. Some older areas have been designated as conservation areas, examples being Bloomsbury and Spitalfields. Marinas have been established in centres with waterfronts and docks, such as St Catherine's Dock.

These developments have also been attractive to more wealthy residents, who have moved near to the city centre. This can be seen in Bloomsbury and the Dockland areas close to Tower Bridge, such as St Catherine's Dock and Butler's Wharf. This is part of the process of re-urbanisation.

Overall, the changes in central areas have turned London into a global 24-hour city. In the Leicester Square and Piccadilly Circus areas of London, the clubs and restaurants are open all day and night to meet the demand from visitors.

Although these examples are all from London, similar examples can be found in any large city in the UK and indeed the MEDW.

You need to:
- know that decentralisation has permitted new opportunities for change in central areas
- know that retailing and offices have been the main functions to change
- know that improvements such as pedestrianisation, conservation areas and gentrification have occurred
- understand that tourism has taken advantage of the changes in a variety of ways
- know that a global 24-hour city has been established
- understand that the changes are frequently linked to re-urbanisation
- know case studies at a small scale and from larger cities

Synoptic links
- Unit 2, element 2
- Unit 5, element 3

Urban deprivation

Decay and deprivation in the UK: causes and characteristics

Deprivation has been defined as when 'an individual's well-being falls below a level generally regarded as a reasonable minimum for Britain today'. In 2000, six groups of indices were used to indicate deprivation. These were:
- income/benefits (9 indices)
- employment (5 indices)
- health, deprivation and disability (5 indices)
- education and skills (6 indices)
- housing (3 indices)
- geographical access to services (5 indices)

Where a number of these groups of indices are found together, the area is said to be experiencing multiple deprivation.

The main areas associated with decay and deprivation in the UK are the inner cities and social housing estates, both in the inner cities and the suburbs.

The causes of the decay are various. In most cases, the housing stock is old and in a state of disrepair as a result of lack of investment in the fabric and poor quality materials used in the housing built after 1945.

The table below shows the characteristics of areas of deprivation compared with areas without deprivation. IC refers to the inner cities and OS to the outer suburbs.

Category	Causes and characteristics of decay and deprivation
Economic	• Lack of investment as funds focused on New Towns (IC) • Decline of traditional industries (IC) • Change in port–trade patterns (IC) • Low-skilled labour failed to attract new service-based employment (IC) (OS)
Social	• Segregation of population — middle-class flight to the suburbs, leaving poorer, lower-class, less-qualified groups (IC) (OS) • From 1960s onwards, segregation by ethnic group — new Commonwealth migrants concentrated in inner-city ghettoes (areas where members of an ethnic, religious or cultural minority are concentrated) (IC) • Most older housing is pre-1914 — may lack bathroom, WC and/or hot water (IC) • Housing shows evidence of overcrowding (IC) • Higher death and infant mortality rates, lower life expectancy and greater incidence of disease (IC) (OS) • More low-income, semi-skilled and manual workers — many on benefits (IC) (OS) • More single-parent families, pensioners, and children in care and/or on free school meals (IC) (OS) • Low level of car ownership and high bus fares increase isolation from shops, employment etc. (IC) (OS) • High levels of unemployment (30%+) (IC) (OS) • Greater incidence of crime and drug abuse (IC) (OS) • Low levels of academic achievement (IC) (OS)
Environmental	• More noise and air pollution (IC) • Derelict land and buildings, with more rubbish (IC) (OS) • Vandalism and graffiti (IC) (OS) • Water courses polluted (IC) (OS) • Deteriorating physical fabric of buildings (IC) (OS) • High-rise buildings engendering feelings of isolation (IC) (OS)

You need to:

- understand what is meant by decay and deprivation
- know the causes and characteristics of decay and deprivation, with reference to the UK
- know where inner-city areas are located
- know the causes and characteristics of a ghetto
- know where areas of peripheral social housing are located
- be familiar with the causes of decline of these areas of deprivation, with reference to the UK
- know the social, economic and environmental characteristics of areas of decay and deprivation

Decay and deprivation: initiatives and policies

In the UK, the stimulus for developing policies to tackle decay and deprivation came after 1945. Policies were framed to deal with a chronic housing shortage, much of which was caused by war damage.

Policies from 1945 to 1979

There were a number of strands during this period. Redevelopment was perhaps the most evident, allied to a general policy of decentralisation from the inner cities. Large areas of nineteenth-century terraced housing had been damaged by bombing and that which remained was considered substandard, often being without a bathroom or inside lavatory. Large areas of all the major conurbations in the UK were redeveloped and replaced by estates, both on existing sites and in the suburbs. The housing types usually included high-rise flats as well as other high-density blocks of apartments. As a rule, the housing plans included some low-density housing in the peripheral estates only. Although there was some movement into private housing, a significant proportion of the decanted population moved to council estates. As a consequence of the transfer of much of this housing type from local authority ownership to housing associations in the 1980s and 90s, this type of accommodation is now referred to as social housing.

A key element of policy was to reduce housing density in the inner areas. Decentralisation of residents displaced by the redevelopment was to suburban estates and to New Towns, which were built on surrounding greenfield sites to take overspill from the large conurbations. Examples from London include redevelopment in Peckham and Deptford and large estates in the Crays, Bromley, on the edge of the conurbation. Similar examples are to be found in any large urban area in the UK.

As well as the clear benefits of these policies, a number of issues became apparent.

Benefits	Issues
• Improved housing conditions; less over-crowding with internal WCs and separate bathrooms • Larger, well-planned properties • Modern housing layouts at a lower density with more open space	• Break-up of existing communities; increased social alienation • Characteristics of deprivation were taken to the new estates, as socioeconomic conditions did not change for all

As a result of these issues, policy changed in the 1960s. As well as redevelopment schemes, urban renewal, with the refurbishment of existing property, became the more favoured approach. This had the advantage of keeping communities together and improving the fabric of the existing building stock.

Policies since 1980

There was a fresh impetus given to inner-city renewal in the 1980s. The Inner City Programme had six aims:
- to improve employment prospects and the ability of local people to compete
- to bring derelict land and buildings into use
- to improve housing conditions
- to encourage self-help
- to improve environmental quality
- to encourage private sector investment in all of the above

A number of strategies were established. The main ones were as follows:
- Grants were available to enable derelict land to be reclaimed. National Garden Festivals were a medium for this.
- Enterprise Zones were established, in which taxes were reduced or abolished, and grants given to companies to enable them to set up businesses more easily.
- Urban development corporations (UDCs) spearheaded initiatives to regenerate large derelict areas. One of the largest schemes was the London Docklands Development Corporation (LDDC), set up in 1981 (see below).
- City Challenge was a scheme in which cities were encouraged to compete to produce the best schemes to improve housing and to encourage industry and employment, gaining finance from the private sector to achieve this.
- The Urban Programme, introduced in 1989, provided 75% grants to the most needy local authorities to tackle the social, economic and environmental problems in their areas.

Recent policies

Since 1990, policies have moved away from competition towards partnerships, a trend accelerated by the change of government in 1997. Many of the initiatives outlined above had 10-year lifespans and therefore change was inevitable. English Partnerships, the main agency, took over the responsibilities of City Grant and Derelict Land Grant in the 1990s. With the merger of the Commission for New Towns and the Urban Regeneration Authority in 2001, it now has responsibility for all urban regeneration, including UDCs, Urban Regeneration Companies, the National Coalfields Programme, Housing Action Trusts (tenants agree to transfer ownership from the local authority to a trust in exchange for government investment) and New Towns. It is responsible for several key areas of activity: housing, strategic brownfield redevelopment and sustainable regeneration.

As well as these government initiatives, funding is available to areas of deprivation from the European Regional Development Fund (ERDF) and the Single Regeneration Budget (SRB), both of which use EU funding streams.

The government also offers grants via small-scale initiatives, including the Neighbourhood Renewal Unit. In addition, education is supported via the Excellence in Cities initiative, which is tackling educational underachievement in the inner cities.

Re-urbanisation and gentrification

These processes play an important role in regeneration. Generally, this is led by the private sector and involves wealthier people moving back into the regenerated areas, usually by refurbishing older property. Examples in London include Islington, Fulham and Chelsea. The conversion of former warehouses in the LDDC area, and the construction of new buildings in similar styles, has caused an influx of the wealthy to be near to the City of London and Canary Wharf for employment. These apartments overlooking the river command very high prices. The result is that poorer residents are driven out, because as the prices increase they are unable to compete for housing. The LDDC's policy of including social housing developments in its area has produced a more balanced social structure (see below), but this is not the case in gentrified areas. The increased segregation results in the urban poor being concentrated outside these areas of gentrification, frequently in areas of social housing or low-quality, private rented accommodation.

You need to:
- know the regeneration policies and strategies as applied to the inner cities
- be aware of the expansion of these strategies into the social housing estates in the suburbs
- understand the changing emphasis of the policies over time
- be familiar with the contribution of re-urbanisation and gentrification to the regeneration of the inner city
- know how these processes affect the urban poor

Policies and strategies: evaluation, values and attitudes

An evaluation of these policies and strategies shows successes and failures, in part depending on the varying perspectives of the different interest groups involved.

The government view

Governments insist that the policies have been successful. Using London Docklands as an example, the evidence for this is the physical regeneration of over 750 hectares of derelict land. This includes the construction of 144 km of new roads, railways (Docklands Light Railway and Jubilee Line extension) and London City airport, as well as improvements to the infrastructure of public utilities (gas, water, electricity and sewerage). In addition, by 1998 nearly £10 billion had been invested (80% by the private sector), resulting in nearly 25 million square metres of commercial and industrial development, a large increase in those employed in the area, from 27 000 to 85 000 in 2700 businesses (1100 in 1981), and 24 000 new homes built.

The housing tenure is more varied, both private, particularly in the areas closer to Tower Bridge, and social, with a greater number of housing units overall to meet this need. There is a greater social mix than before. Social infrastructure has been supported with five new health centres (and improvements to another six), 11 new primary and two new secondary schools, three post-16 colleges and nine vocational training centres. In addition, retailing has been regenerated, with new supermarkets, such as Jubilee Place at Canary Wharf, and many types of restaurant.

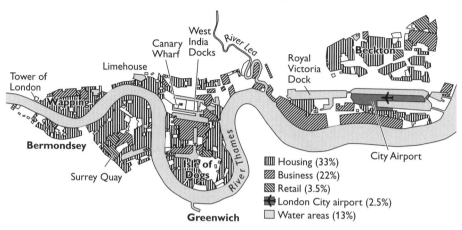

Housing (33%)
Business (22%)
Retail (3.5%)
London City airport (2.5%)
Water areas (13%)

Since 1998, six new tower office blocks have been constructed at Canary Wharf, further increasing the relevant figures quoted above. In addition, 23 000 new jobs have been created in central London as a result of the increase in supply of high-grade office accommodation, producing a more competitive financial centre.

It is clear that only an organisation, such as a UDC, has the economic and political drive to ensure that change occurs on the necessary scale. This can be seen in all UDCs, including Cardiff Bay, which is still in operation.

The critics' evaluation

Critics argue from a number of points of view. The new employment opportunities tended to be in services, requiring skills that those made unemployed (12 000 from the docks alone between 1978 and 1983) did not have, necessitating retraining. Many of the new jobs in the LDDC area were relocated from other areas of London and did not offer employment opportunities to the local inhabitants. Existing communities were broken up as people moved out to allow redevelopment to take place or to find alternative employment.

Much of the residential stock went to wealthier in-migrants, especially close to Tower Bridge. Local people were unable to compete for such accommodation and social segregation increased in some areas as many developments were enclosed and gated.

Values and attitudes

The ability to assess values and attitudes is an essential tool for a geography student. This is particularly so when considering areas of decay and deprivation. The specification requires you to consider your own values and attitudes and those of decision makers.

If you live in a rural area, your perception of areas of decay and deprivation is likely to be different from that of someone who lives in such an area. Your image of an area of deprivation may be influenced by your experiences and by the perception you gain from the media. A news item may make generalisations about such areas based on a localised issue. This could be far from the reality experienced by those living just a few hundred metres away. Does a negative view of such areas perpetuate the issues or does it lead to greater understanding?

When you are evaluating strategies and policies, do your solutions and views differ from the responsible government agency and/or from those living there? An evaluation of government policy may be influenced by your own political views or those of others. These are just some of the considerations you could take into account when evaluating issues in geography.

You need to:
- be able to give a case study of an urban development corporation (UDC)
- evaluate the success of strategies and policies used to tackle decay and deprivation
- understand the importance of attitudes and values (both yours and those of others) when evaluating such strategies and policies

Synoptic links
- Unit 2, element 2
- Unit 5, element 1

Urban deprivation in the LEDW: shanty towns

Shanty towns are a feature of most cities in the LEDW. They have grown up as a consequence of rapid urbanisation, resulting from migration into the city and high rates of population increase. The location of shanties varies. In many cities, they are found on the periphery of the urban area, being established at the point where new migrants reach the city. They are found on any available land that is not occupied by other uses; thus, they are usually illegal settlements. For example, in Rio de Janeiro, Brazil, they occupy slopes that are too steep for other functions and are susceptible to landslides or flash floods. In Nairobi, shanties occur on swampland; in Cairo they occur in the cemetery area — the 'City of the Dead'.

As cities grow, newer shanties are found increasingly further from the centre, causing transport problems for those forced to travel to work in other parts of the city. Thus, in many cities, there is a pattern in which the age of the shanty decreases from the centre of the urban area.

The characteristics of shanty towns include:
- housing built from any local materials
- lack of basic infrastructure (e.g. water, sewerage, electricity)
- shortage of medical facilities, schools and other public services
- contaminated drinking water, so diseases such as cholera, typhoid and dysentery are common
- few pollution controls on local industry, leading to contaminated water supplies, poor air quality and respiratory diseases

- high levels of unemployment and underemployment; many survive by working in the informal sector at, or near to, subsistence level

Shanty towns are a product of regional imbalances, as the city acts as a magnet to people. The attractions of the city outweigh the disadvantages of the shanty environment and are a reflection of a dynamic local economy experiencing rapid economic growth. Thus, it can be said that shanty towns are a benefit to the national and local economy. They have been described as 'cities of hope' because of the opportunities offered to those living in them.

There have been a number of initiatives in different parts of the LEDW to improve the lot of shanty dwellers. These are outlined in the following table.

Initiative	Details	Evaluation
Demolition	Policy in South Africa and Brazil many years ago; illegal settlements were cleared by force	Only a temporary effect; the displaced residents had to live somewhere, usually nearby, and others returned to the same sites
Site and service	Although reluctant, governments have found it more expedient to work with residents; the residents build the housing and the government provides the essential basic services (e.g. water, drainage, building materials, electricity and roads); schools and healthcare facilities may be added; an example is the periferia of São Paulo (Brazil)	Successful and value for money; the enthusiasm and drive of the local people is harnessed and supported so that the quality of both the housing and the area is improved
Cooperatives	In Lusaka (Zambia) groups of 25 or so people are encouraged to form a cooperative; they are given a water supply and land; water and drainage pipes are laid in exchange for their labour; building materials are supplied if the labour supply is maintained	Successful in parts of the LEDW in providing housing for a large number of people
Self-help	Applied in Nairobi (Kenya); the local government provided basic amenities and building materials at a low price; wealthier people bought the plots of land and built a number of houses; local government provided water, sewerage, electricity and roads; surplus housing was sold off	Successful on a large scale (120 000 people live in the area of this initiative); the very poor have been excluded

Initiative	Details	Evaluation
High-rise blocks	Most effective in Singapore; older property was demolished and estates (for 10 000–30 000 people) were built in the form of high-rise blocks of flats; the blocks were arranged to form new towns (250 000 people); the residents used their savings to purchase their flats; transport to the city centre is by light railway	Accommodation on a large scale in well-planned environments; local industrial employment established at the same time
New settlements	Hong Kong and Caracas (Venezuela), which are more developed, have constructed new towns away from the city centre	Successful in housing large numbers of people in high-rise blocks; rapid transit systems have been constructed to connect with the city centre
Satellite settlements	Five satellite towns are being constructed in the desert outside Cairo (Egypt)	Successfully rehousing people in large numbers; the provision of employment in the satellites is inadequate; commuting has increased, causing pressure on transport links

In most cases, the housing provision fails to keep up with the rapid population increase, so is of limited success overall. Singapore has low population growth and so is more successful from this point-of-view.

You need to:
- know the growth, location and characteristics of shanty towns
- understand the importance of shanty towns as a consequence of rapid economic growth
- be familiar with the range of initiatives to improve housing conditions in shanty towns
- evaluate the initiatives undertaken to improve housing conditions in shanty towns

Synoptic links
- Unit 2, element 2
- Unit 5, elements 1 and 3

Environmental issues

Urban pollution and associated health risks

Urban areas have been associated with air, water and land pollution for centuries and, consequentially, with high mortality rates. The main types of pollution and the associated health risks are set out below.

Pollution type	Source	Health risk
Smog	Industrial and residential smoke and vehicle exhaust emissions in the form of microscopic particles coalesce with water vapour to form smoke fog, particularly under inversion conditions (see Unit 1 Guide in this series)	Respiratory diseases, including asthma, are exacerbated, causing breathing difficulties and increasing mortality rates In countries with coal-based economies, smog is the main source of urban air pollution In the MEDW, where air pollution controls are in place, photochemical smog is more important
Low-level ozone	Vehicle exhaust emissions (e.g. SO_2 and NO_2) react with sunlight to produce ozone at low levels in the urban atmosphere, particularly under inversion conditions	
Lead pollution	Product of car exhaust emissions; particularly con-centrated in locations with high traffic flows	High lead concentrations have a serious impact on brain development in children In the MEDW, lead has been removed from gasoline for cars
Noise	A variety of sources, e.g. traffic, aircraft, industrial processes and people's activities	Effects on health include persistent sleep deprivation, hearing impairment and noise rage In the MEDW, legal restrictions on noise levels and enforcement are in place
Water pollution	Mainly a result of industrial effluent and sewage being discharged into rivers and streams	Water-borne diseases such as cholera; toxic pollution causing deformities in babies and young children Common in the LEDW, where no restrictions on industry are in place and there is a lack of sewerage systems; in the MEDW, controls are in place and the issue is of less concern
Land pollution	Mainly a result of land contaminated by industrial processes, e.g. gas works, metal processing, chemical processes	Poisons and toxic wastes produced by these processes remain in the soil, causing poisoning and, in addition, deformities in babies and young children Contamination makes it difficult for other forms of land use to follow In the MEDW, reclamation of land is possible, but problems may arise for people later if housing is constructed on the land and pollutants rise to the surface

You need to:
- know the types of urban pollution related to air, water and land sources
- know the health risks related to these types of pollution

- be familiar with the spatial variations in the impact of, and response to, these types of pollution

The issue of waste disposal

Urban populations produce huge amounts of waste, especially in the MEDW. The disposal of this waste, both in the LEDW and MEDW, raises a number of issues.

Taking the UK as an example from the MEDW, there are several methods of waste disposal, each with its own issues.

Landfill

Commercial and domestic waste is buried in disused quarries and pits. This method is relatively cheap and the land can be subsequently reclaimed for other uses.

Issues arising include:
- pollution of the underlying water table by leaching
- leaking of gases after reclamation
- contamination of crops and gardens
- subsidence of buildings on the site after a number of years

Strategies used in the UK include:
- sealing the base and top of the landfill with clay and/or a waterproof plastic membrane to:
  - prevent leaching
  - reduce the escape of gases
  - reduce the probability of contamination of the overlying land
- imposing controls on the type of waste dumped to reduce the pollution hazard, though these are difficult to enforce
- reducing subsidence by using stronger foundations and then restricting the types of buildings (e.g. the regional shopping centre at Merry Hill near Dudley is built on reclaimed industrial land; it would have been more difficult to gain planning permission for housing)
- imposing landfill tax to encourage a decrease in the amount of waste disposed and to encourage recycling initiatives

Incineration

Waste is burned in specialised facilities. There is potential for release into the atmosphere of toxic gases such as dioxins, as well as carbon dioxide. This causes concern for local residents.

In the UK:
- waste must be burned at very high temperatures to ensure that all toxins are neutralised
- some incinerators have been built as combined heat and power units and supply hot water to nearby residents (e.g. Deptford, London)
- few sites are given planning permission

Dumping at sea

This involves transporting waste (commonly industrial, toxic metals) in barges and dumping it at sea. The release of such toxic waste into the oceanic food chain is cause for concern. This practice is banned by the EU.

Disposal in water

This is the direct release of industrial waste and sewage into watercourses and the sea. This contaminates the aquatic ecosystem as well as beaches and other tourist facilities. If nitrates are released, aquatic life may increase.

Under EU legislation, untreated waste cannot be released into watercourses.

Underground disposal

Toxic waste can be buried in deep mines and/or shafts and sealed in. This approach is used for the most toxic wastes, such as radioactive material. The risk of escape is reduced, but not prevented, and leakage to the water table is the main concern.

In the UK, radioactive material is buried at Sellafield, in Cumbria, under strict controls.

Whatever the type of waste disposal in use or suggested in the MEDW, all have environmental impact and concerns. Every new scheme raises environmental objections. Current policy is to reduce the amount of waste by recycling, more efficient use of materials and taxation. The aim is to use a combination of strategies to reduce the threats to urban (and other) ecosystems.

In the LEDW, waste disposal is mostly unregulated and environmental damage is much greater than in the MEDW. In some cities, many people make a living by recycling waste by hand, in some cases living on the large waste tips on the outskirts of cities.

You need to:
- know the main types of waste disposal
- know the issues arising from each type of disposal
- be familiar with the strategies employed to reduce the environmental impact
- understand the threats posed to urban ecosystems by waste disposal
- be aware of the spatial variations in the quality of urban life in the LEDW and the MEDW

Urban conservation projects

The environment in urban areas can be protected and enhanced by conservation. Designated conservation areas, within which a group of architecturally important buildings are conserved, protect the built environment. There are restrictions on external (and internal, if listed) alterations to the buildings, with the aim of keeping the environment as it is. Many old town centres, such as Canterbury (Kent) and Rye (Sussex), are conservation areas.

The natural environment can be enhanced by conservation projects that try to return the polluted urban environment to a natural, healthy state. This can cover water and/or land pollution and conservation projects vary in scale from very small to large.

For example, the River Lea in London has been cleaned up. The water is less polluted because industry has declined and pollution sources have reduced. Flora, such as reeds and water plants, have been planted and appropriate fauna encouraged and introduced. At a smaller scale, a square in a town centre can be replanted and birdlife encouraged. This has been carried out in several parts of central London, for example in Russell and Soho Squares.

You need to:

- understand the role of conservation projects in the natural and built environments

Containing growth

In the MEDW, unrestricted urban growth is considered to be inappropriate and a number of strategies have been used to control such expansion.

Green belts were first fully established in the UK after 1945. The unrestricted growth of London up until the Second World War had produced urban sprawl as the suburbs expanded without planning controls.

The London green belt was a band of green (undeveloped) land around London within which development was strongly controlled or prevented. Any future urban growth and development was to be channelled into the eight New Towns and expanded towns. This was allied to the policy of decentralisation, which was in place until 1980.

Advantages	Disadvantages
• Rural land was protected from urban development	• The cost of land rose inside the green belt
• Urban populations could access the green belt land for recreation	• Longer journeys to work
• Higher quality housing in purpose-built development	• Increasing use of private cars
• Self-contained towns with local employment, reducing the need for commuting	• Urban pressures leapfrog the green belt and are not contained
• Brownfield land used for urban development	• Housing shortages in the urban area
	• M25 built in green belt, increasing developmental pressure

Other major conurbations, cities and towns in the UK established their own green belts to prevent sprawl. Development was forced outside; most had their own New Towns in the surrounding area. Population decline in the main conurbations (other than London, which has seen population increase in recent years) has meant reduced urban pressure. For example, there are over 100 000 empty houses in cities in the north of England, whereas in the southeast there is a shortage and there is a need for 670 000 more homes by 2021. This demand has arisen because of the increase in the number of households (200 000 each year) in the UK, as a result of divorce, longevity and more people choosing to live alone.

Other strategies have been used to achieve similar ends. Channelling growth into sectors, frequently along transport arteries, has allowed **green wedges** to be retained. The concentration of planned growth along the lower Thames is an example of this, leaving the green belt areas undeveloped.

In the Netherlands, urban areas virtually form a circle, leaving a **green heart** in the middle. This area has been protected in the same way as the green belt in the UK.

Thus, it is policy in many countries in the MEDW to ensure that green buffers are established to prevent unrestricted urban growth totally covering the landscape with development.

You need to:
- understand the importance of green belts, wedges and hearts in urban planning
- know examples of green belts, wedges and hearts in the UK and the EU
- know the advantages and disadvantages of green belts, wedges and hearts

Spatial variations in the quality of urban life

Planning considerations have an impact on the development of cities. In particular, they can increase and/or reduce spatial inequalities in cities, inequalities that are based on economic, social and environmental processes. The attitudes and values of decision makers play an important part in the ways in which their decisions affect these inequalities. Wealthier people wish to live in green areas, and have the financial means to do so. This limits the choice of location for the less well off.

You are required to explore your own values and attitudes with regard to spatial varia-tions in the quality of urban life. Some questions you should consider include, 'Where do I live?' and 'Where do I want to live in the future?'

You need to:
- know the spatial variations in the quality of urban life
- understand the economic, social and environmental processes influencing these variations
- appreciate the role of the attitudes and values of decision makers in relation to urban issues
- evaluate your own attitudes and values in relation to these issues

Synoptic links

- Unit 1, elements 2 and 3
- Unit 2, elements 2 and 3
- Unit 5, element 3

Recreation and tourism

The resource base

Recreation and tourism: definitions and classification

Recreation ('leisure' in this context) and tourism together form one of the most impor-tant service industries, accounting for around 10% of global output. Recreation is defined as activities undertaken voluntarily in one's own time, which may be under-taken at home. Tourism involves visiting places and utilising planned commercial activities. Tourism includes trips taken for leisure purposes as well as for business, health and religious reasons.

Tourist activities are classified by the types of resource to be found:
- Primary resources are natural and historical. These include the scenery, the climate, the ecology and historical/heritage sites (in summary, the attractions in the area that are not specifically provided for tourists).
- Secondary resources are those specifically provided to meet the needs of tourists. These include accommodation, catering, hospitality, entertainment, education, tourist infrastructure (travel agents, transport facilities, guides) and theme parks.

Many areas involved in tourism have both primary and secondary resources, though the balance varies. High-intensity areas have a dominance of secondary resources. Examples include theme parks (e.g. Disneyland Paris) and urban recreational areas (e.g. Lea Valley and theatre-land in the West End of London). Average-intensity areas have a balance between primary and secondary resources. Examples include coastal resorts, where there is both natural scenery and built attractions (e.g. Brighton and Blackpool). Low-intensity areas have a dominance of primary resources. Examples include National Parks in the UK, such as the Lake District and the Peak District.

You need to:

- be able to define recreation and tourism
- be able to classify tourism resources
- give examples of the balance between primary and secondary resources

Tourism resources: contrasts, capacity and application

Although there are contrasts between the LEDW and the MEDW with regard to primary and secondary tourist resources, in many cases the differences are far from clear. For example, there is a tendency for the most developed secondary tourist infrastructure to be in the MEDW, with primary resources being more important in the LEDW. However, tourists will not visit the primary resources in the LEDW, such as safari parks, if the secondary resources, such as hotels and transport required to support the visit, are not in place.

This distinction is also valid at a regional/national scale, with the more scenic areas of the UK having more emphasis on primary resources (with secondary resources provided) in comparison with the main tourist resources in many urban areas, which are mainly secondary.

The capacity of a tourist resource can be assessed using a range of criteria.

Criterion	Assessment
Physical	There are physical limits to the numbers of visitors that can be in or at a tourist facility without causing danger to the tourists or damage to the environment Numbers can be controlled by the use of tickets or by limiting the number of vehicles allowed access
Ecological/ environmental	Visitors can cause ecological damage if numbers are not controlled Damage might include footpath erosion, habitat destruction, pollution and damage to routeways by vehicles, or the physical erosion of pavements and buildings in high-intensity areas
Economic	This is the maximum amount of money that can be generated by a tourist facility
Perceived	People's perception of the capacity of a tourist area will influence their decision on whether to visit; if the perception is that the facility will be overcrowded, then the visit may not take place The perception may be independent of the physical capacity; for example, a rural facility with 100 visitors might be considered overcrowded, whereas in a purpose-built secondary facility, many thousands of visitors can be accommodated without the perception of capacity being exceeded

The study at a local scale of a tourist area or facility will enable the distinction between types of resource to be explored or the various capacities to be assessed. The assessment of changes over time should also be applied to the case study.

You need to:
- understand the contrasts in tourist resources between the LEDW and the MEDW
- know the capacities of tourist resources and how they can be assessed
- carry out a local study to distinguish between tourist resources and know how they have changed over time

Synoptic links

- Unit 1, element 2
- Unit 2, elements 2 and 3
- Unit 5, element 1

Boom in the MEDW

The theoretical base: Butler's model

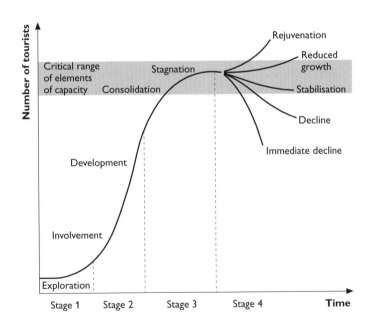

This model shows the theoretical stages of development of a tourist area. It can be applied to almost any such area or facility. Mallorca is frequently quoted with reference to this model, the stages being as follows:
- Stage 1 (exploration) is the initial discovery of a tourist destination, often used by an elite, and experiencing slow growth. During the twentieth century until the 1950s, Mallorca was in this stage. The primary resources of sandy beaches, mountains and cliffs, warm climate and medieval buildings made the island attractive to writers, artists and the rich.

- Stage 2 (involvement/development) is accelerated growth, as the destination becomes more accessible and widely known. The 1960s saw the rapid development of secondary tourist facilities for the cheap, mass-market holidaymaker. Rising prosperity, cheap airfares and package tours resulted in the building of high-rise hotels and much unplanned growth, which damaged the environment.
- Stage 3 (consolidation/stagnation) is the stage of maturity, when the destination's popularity stagnates or declines. By 1990, Mallorca's tourist industry was stagnant. Mass tourism was declining as the island was considered to be downmarket and newer locations were favoured.
- Stage 4 is future development. Some areas reinvent themselves; others decline and lose their tourist function. Rejuvenation in Mallorca was set in place by an emphasis on the natural environment, culture and golf. This was intended to appeal to the more discerning visitor and there is now a better balance for the various types of holidaymaker.

An example from the UK is Hastings. Stage 1 was from the late eighteenth century to the mid-nineteenth century. The wealthy travelled from London for the primary resources of the sea, the beach, the harbour and the old town. Stage 2 came with the railway. This enabled mass tourism to take place and secondary resources, such as hotels, guesthouses and cafés, as well as the pier and theatre, were constructed. Stage 3 was reached by the 1960s, though some consider that stagnation occurred earlier. Visitors went to other resorts and facilities, usually abroad, and there was a clear shift from weekly stays to daytrips as the town became unfashionable. In Stage 4, Hastings has struggled to stabilise and may still be declining. Examples of rejuvenation are few and far between, despite the best efforts of the authorities.

In summary, the causes of the growth of tourism (both in the MEDW and the LEDW) are physical, economic, sociological and technological. They include the growth in personal income, increased leisure time, paid holidays, a shorter working week, earlier retirement, increased mobility, improved and cheaper transport (e.g. Easyjet), package holidays, greater awareness of different cultures and locations, changing fashions, international use of technology and IT (credit cards, e-tickets) and better and more reliable climates at the chosen destinations. A relative rise in the pound sterling against the euro in the early twenty-first century also made European holidays good value for money.

You need to:
- know the theoretical basis, i.e. Butler's model
- know two case studies of the growth of tourism, including one from the UK, at a resort and regional scale
- understand the theoretical development of a tourist resort
- know the causes of the growth of tourism

Recent changes in tourism in the MEDW

In recent years there has been a change in the relative importance of tourist destinations. Within the UK, short breaks have become more popular. Longer holidays are usually taken abroad. Increasingly, within the Mediterranean region, there has been a shift away from Spain towards Greece, Cyprus, Turkey and Tunisia. As technology reduces the costs of travel, the USA (Florida and California), the Gulf and the Far East are also gaining in importance. The wealthier now travel to more exotic locations, including Central and South America, Antarctica, Australia, eastern and southern Africa and New Zealand.

Activity holidays are also increasing in popularity. These can be in the UK (e.g. Center Parcs) or abroad (e.g. white-water rafting in Turkey). Purpose-built resorts, such as Center Parcs, and theme parks, such as Disneyland Paris, Portaventura (Barcelona), Disney World (Florida) and Alton Towers (UK), are increasingly popular, for both daytrips and longer stays, as appropriate.

Another increasingly popular type of holiday, usually for short breaks, is urban tourism. This could be a visit to Albert Dock in Liverpool, a weekend in London, with all the heritage, culture and entertainment on offer, or a city break to a European city, such as Paris, Madrid, Prague or Rome. Shopping trips to New York or Boston are also popular and, as the pound has risen against the dollar, more accessible.

You need to:
- be familiar with the recent changes in tourist destinations in the MEDC in terms of timing, length of stay and type
- be aware of the increase in urban tourism, theme parks and activity holidays

Synoptic links
- Unit 2, elements 2 and 3
- Unit 4, element 3
- Unit 5, element 2

Expansion in the LEDW

Reasons for the growth of tourism in the LEDW

Primary tourist resources are very important in the LEDW and have long been attractive to the more adventurous traveller. The range of primary resources is extremely wide, and includes unspoilt scenery, wild animals, natural vegetation and ancient buildings such as the Taj Mahal, Machu Picchu and the pyramids.

In the late twentieth century, the construction and establishment of secondary resources, including transport infrastructure, hotels, package tours, and the falling costs of air travel, have encouraged many more people to travel to the LEDW.

In recent years, Kenya has been one of the main tourist destinations in Africa. Inland attractions include the safari parks (Masai Mara is perhaps the most renowned) and unique landscapes in the Rift Valley. Safaris are a popular tourist experience. On the coasts there are coral reefs in the marine parks, with opportunities for diving and fishing, as well as other water sports. As the secondary infrastructure has been established, purpose-built resorts have been constructed. These include the Turtle Bay Beach Club and Voyager Beach Resort (Mombasa) in the north and Southern Palms and Diani Sea Resort in the south. All have them have pools, bars, watersports and so on.

In Cuba, development has been in the form of enclaves (coastal planned resorts). A good example of this is Varadero, on the northwest coast, with its beaches and warm, tropical climate. Secondary resources include a five-star Sandals hotel with three pools, sports and leisure facilities, water sports and a nightclub. A four-star hotel is nearby, with similar facilities. Both are 'inclusive' hotels. This reinforces the enclave mentality, as tourists do not have to leave the resort for any activities, though some go on excursions to Havana. The Cuban government favours such development because the generation of income is focused. In addition, the infrastructure is easier and cheaper to provide and the visitors do not mix too much with local people, reflecting the political control the government holds in Cuba. There is some small-scale trade in local crafts.

Both the above examples demonstrate the nature of the industry as a process in the development of globalisation. Tourism takes place because of the growth of TNCs such as Thomson (Tui) and Thomas Cook. These corporations are able to offer holidays to the large market in the MEDW, using hotel facilities also owned by TNCs, such as Sandals, Movenpick and Riu. The airlines flying the tourists are also TNCs, such as Britannia (Tui), British Airways or British West Indian Airways. In addition, the car hire companies, such as Europcar, Dollar and Hertz, are TNCs.

You need to:
- understand the reasons for the growth of tourism in the LEDW (see the MEDW section)
- give two case studies to show understanding of this growth
- know the factors stimulating demand (see the MEDW section)
- be familiar with patterns of growth in coastal planned resorts and inland developments
- understand the role of TNCs in the industry

Synoptic links
- Unit 1, element 2

Tourism and the environment

The use of primary resources

The growth of the tourist industry has been dependent on primary tourist resources. These tend to be scenic and/or historical. The development of the resource results in environmental impact or damage, with associated conflicts and issues. The development of secondary tourist resources increases the impact and damage, and intensifies many of the conflicts and issues.

In order to control and minimise the environmental impact, management strategies have been developed and applied. National Parks in the UK have a number of different interest groups with a stake in the environment. The Parks are charged with conserving and enhancing their special qualities and providing opportunities for people to enjoy and understand them.

The management of the Peak District National Park, for example, is based on two principles, sustainable development and partnership. The concept of sustainable development is applicable in other environments and means meeting today's needs without damaging the Park or preventing future generations from using and enjoying it. Partnerships involve working with organisations such as local authorities, government agencies, environmental groups, community groups, land owners, education providers, recreational interests, economic organisations, and utilities and transport interests, as well as the public, to achieve sustainable development.

Tourists and tourism provide both opportunities and challenges. For example, 52% of employment in the Peak District is in services (including tourism). Twenty-two million visitor days per annum cause great pressure on the Park, especially when the tourism is unmanaged. Most tourists (90%) come by car. An integrated traffic management strategy proposes use of traffic calming and reduced cross-Park traffic on main roads.

Greater access under 'Freedom to Roam' legislation will enhance issues such as footpath erosion, maintenance of paths and tracks, effects on wildlife and conflicts between walkers and other users. Access management strategies include reducing dependency on cars and encouraging cycling and walking, promoting public transport (including rail in the Hope Valley), increasing the number of park-and-ride schemes, containing and managing car parking, piloting road pricing schemes and restricting car access to certain heavily used sites.

In recent years, the range of recreational activity and organised sports has increased and now includes climbing, caving, cycling, riding, orienteering, fell running, angling, off-road driving and hang gliding.

Tourist activities are widespread in the Park, but there are concentrations of pressure, particularly in the Hope Valley and at Castleton. Management strategies are working to manage the demand in these areas, in order to permit the less popular areas to remain relatively unspoilt. The development of facilities such as car parks, park-and-ride schemes, hotels, restaurants, picnic areas, toilets and shops in 'honeypots' enables this. Major pathways, such as the Pennine Way, are carefully maintained with permanent surfaces and step replacement.

Conservation projects support farmers, landscape managers and communities, with regard to landscape, buildings and economic activities. In addition, biodiversity is maintained and pollution managed.

You need to:
- be aware of the use of primary tourist resources
- understand the environmental impact and damage associated with tourism

- be aware of the conflicts arising from tourism
- be aware of the management strategies employed to reduce the impact of tourism
- know a case study of a National Park in the UK

Primary tourist resources: wilderness areas

Wilderness areas are identified as having little or no human interference or management of natural systems. In a densely populated area such as England, these areas are unlikely to exist, whereas in less populated and remote areas, such as Alaska or Antarctica, they are readily identified. They are formally and legally identified in the USA, where no attempt is made to allow access to the public (e.g. Glacier Peak Wilderness, Washington State).

You need to:
- understand the concept and identification of wilderness areas

Primary tourist resources: ecotourism

Ecotourism is the opposite of mass tourism. It involves small numbers of people visiting ecological and human resources such as wildlife, scenic landscapes, traditional cultures and heritage. It is intended to be sustainable and have limited impact on the environment, though this is not always the case.

Costa Rica, in Central America, is a location for ecotourism development. The basis is sightseeing in rainforests, mountain and volcanic environments, but there is some small-scale development around beach resorts. Hotels are owned by local people and are small, usually having less than 100 rooms. Facilities are provided to minimise environmental impact, with renewable building materials and food and drink derived locally wherever possible. Energy use is restricted to the absolute minimum. Conditions might be considered spartan compared with secondary tourist resources in other parts of the world, but those undertaking this type of visit see this as acceptable. At present, ecotourism generates 9% of Costa Rica's GDP.

Sustainability is an important element of ecotourism, and is indeed an intrinsic underpinning theme. The aims of sustainable tourism are to improve the quality of life of the host community, to provide a memorable experience for visitors and to maintain the richness of the environment upon which tourism depends.

You should consider your attitudes and values towards ecotourism. Would you wish to go on a holiday to Costa Rica's ecotourist areas instead of a Mediterranean resort? You could set out your responses in a table to enable you to reach a reasoned conclusion.

You need to:
- be able to define ecotourism
- understand the concept of sustainability as applied to ecotourism
- explore your own attitudes and values in relation to ecotourism

Environmental impact of tourism in the LEDW

There are a number of potential environmental impacts of tourism in the LEDW. These are assessed in the following table.

Impact	Costs	Benefits
Biodiversity	Loss of diversity in plant and animal species by trampling and removal of habitat	Conservation areas and parks help to maintain diversity
Erosion	Removal of plant cover on slopes leads to soil erosion	Strategies to conserve vegetation cover and to manage human impact are established
Pollution	Construction of large-scale secondary tourist resources may lead to sewage treatment problems, waste disposal issues and air pollution	Management strategies are in place; sewerage works are established, waste disposal systems set up and employment in these activities increased
Water supply	Water demand increases rapidly; in coastal areas this can cause the lowering of the water table and saline pollution of groundwater	Local people may benefit from the installation of improved water supplies
Visual impact	Loss of natural vegetation Unplanned secondary tourist facilities	Conservation projects established More sensitive town planning

You need to:
- know the costs and benefits of the environmental impact of tourism in the LEDW

Synoptic links
- Unit 1, element 3
- Unit 4, elements 1 and 3
- Unit 5, element 1

Tourism and development

Economic impacts of tourism

These are evaluated in the following table.

Impact	Costs	Benefits
Investment	Funding is external, so profits are returned to investing countries (leakage)	Foreign currency is earned for the country Capital funding of secondary facilities and modern infrastructure

Impact	Costs	Benefits
Employment	Higher-level posts are filled by foreign workers Vulnerable to changes in the pattern and volume of tourism	Tourism is labour intensive Many jobs are created at various levels and in a number of related services
Taxes	Too high a level of taxes will put off visitors	Income provided for home government
Wages	Wages are often low Employment may be seasonal	Stimulate the local economy (farming/food supply, transport and hotel/attraction services) via the multiplier effect Help to diversify local/regional employment

You need to:
- know the economic costs and benefits of tourism in both the MEDW and the LEDW

Social and cultural impacts of tourism

The social and cultural impacts of tourism are complex and wide-ranging.

Impact	Costs	Benefits
Interaction	Dilution of the local culture Breakdown of traditional lifestyle	Greater understanding of local cultures
Social projects	Exploitation of local people in, for example, the sex industry	Modernisation of, and investment in, schools and health clinics
Health	Greater spread of disease, including AIDs	Improved facilities for local people

You need to:
- know the social and cultural costs and benefits of tourism in both the MEDW and the LEDW

Tourism and economic development

Tourism has the potential to play a major role in the economic development of a country. Many countries have used tourism to stimulate the economy at local, regional and national levels. Governments have promoted this stimulus by allowing the economy to expand of its own accord and by directly encouraging growth by the implementation of planning policies.

The latter approach is based on the concept of growth poles. This strategy involves the concentration of tourist activities in certain defined locations and allowing these to lead economic growth, initially at these poles and subsequently by spreading into the rest of the country. The government in Tunisia has established tourism in a small number of locations, both on the coast and inland, each with appropriate secondary tourist infrastructure.

The expectation is that the economic growth generated by the tourist industry will initiate further growth and spread to other sectors of the economy, a process known as **trickle-down**. The idea of the multiplier, that money spent in the economy circulates and increases economic development, based on **Myrdal's cumulative causation**, is important here. For example, the money invested in a manufacturing plant creates employment in the plant itself and for the component suppliers. The resulting wages are spent and thus support other manufacturing industry and services to meet the needs of the workers. This growth then permits the economy to 'take off' as per **Rostow's model**.

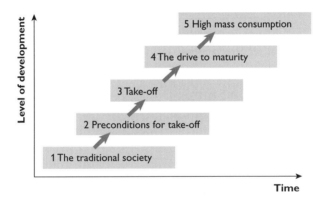

Stage	Name	Characteristics
(1)	Traditional society	• Subsistence economy based on farming • Limited technology and capital
(2)	Preconditions for take-off	• Usually triggered by investment from abroad • Extractive industry, more commercialised farming, transport develops and a single industry tends to dominate • Investment is up to 5% of GNP
(3)	Take-off	• Manufacturing industries grow rapidly and transport infra-structure develops • Growth restricted to one or two areas of the country (growth poles) and one or two industries • Farming employment declines • Investment is between 10% and 15% of GDP
(4)	Drive to maturity	• Growth is self-sustaining • Economic growth spreads to all parts of the country, with an increase in number and types of industry (multiplier effect) • Early industries decline
(5)	Age of high mass consumption	• Rapid expansion of the service sector and welfare facilities • Manufacturing employment declines • Industry dependent on consumer goods

There is potential for economic benefit to many countries as the importance of tourism in the economy increases. Spain, among others, has shown how this can be achieved.

However, the establishment of tourist enclaves and areas over-dependent on tourism can lead to regional economic imbalance. The growth in the tourist areas can cause decline in other areas, to meet the needs of the expanding economy. The migration of workers from other areas could cause both a decline in traditional activities, including farming, and a shortage of labour. It is hoped that the economic development of the tourist area will follow that of the core–periphery model, resulting in the initial concentration of economic activity in the core, which then spreads to the periphery over time.

In addition, there is the issue of over-dependence on tourism, which, if there is a change in the popularity of the tourist area, may result in decline, for example the impact on tourism in Bali after the terrorist bombing.

Tourism is a truly global industry and an excellent example of global interdependence. The increased emphasis on consideration for the environment, including sustainable tourism and ecotourism, and the increase in heritage-based holidays, means that the attitudes and values of those involved in decision-making are of increasing importance. You should examine your own attitudes and values with regard to the issues associated with tourism.

You need to:
- understand the importance of tourism in the establishment of growth poles of national development
- understand the importance of tourism in economic development, including Rostow's and Myrdal's ideas
- know the role of tourism in unequal development
- be aware of the importance of values and attitudes in relation to tourism issues

Synoptic links
- Unit 5, elements 1 and 2

Questions
&
Answers

THE HENLEY COLLEGE LIBRARY

This concluding section of the guide contains three typical resource-based questions (Section A) and three essay questions (Section B), based on the topic areas outlined in the Content Guidance section.

Please note that in the examination you will have to answer two resource-based questions and one essay from those set.

Model answers are given after the questions. These are provided at a typical grade-C standard (Candidate A) and a good grade-A standard (Candidate B).

Examiner's comments

These are preceded by the icon *e*. They are interspersed in the answers and indicate where credit is due. In the weaker answers, they also point out areas for improvement, specific problems and common errors such as poor time management, lack of clarity, weak or non-existent development, irrelevance, misinterpretation of the question and mistaken meanings of terms.

In Section A, parts (a) and (b), marks are awarded by points. In Section A, part (c) and in Section B, marks are awarded by Level (see pages 8–9).

Section A (part (c))	Section B
Level 1: 1–3 marks	Level 1: 1–6 marks
Level 2: 4–5 marks	Level 2: 7–12 marks
Level 3: 6–7 marks	Level 3: 13–18 marks
	Level 4: 19–24 marks
	Level 5: 25–30 marks

Section A

Population pressure and resource management

Question 1

(a) **Distinguish between renewable and non-renewable resources.** (4 marks)

(b) **Outline the ways in which the life of non-renewable resources can be extended.** (4 marks)

(c) **Discuss why the exploitation of a renewable resource, such as timber or water, continues to give cause for concern.** (7 marks)

■ ■ ■

Answer to question 1: Candidate A

(a) Renewable resources are those that are not used up, whereas non-renewable resources are finite and can be exhausted.

> ℓ The candidate has correctly identified the terms at a simple level and distinguished between them. No examples have been given, however, so this response gains only 2 marks.

(b) The life of non-renewable resources can be extended in several ways. These include recycling, better use of the resource, and the discovery of greater reserves and more efficient extraction of the reserves. A good example of this is oil in the North Sea.

> ℓ There is some knowledge of the ways of extending these resources. However, although correct, the methods are listed, rather than outlined. This response gains 2 of the 4 marks as, despite citing an example, it is undeveloped.

(c) Today, timber resources are being continually exploited across the globe and this is causing concern. The rainforests are being cut down at such a rate that an area the size of Wales is destroyed each year. This causes soil erosion, as well as exhausting the soil minerals so that further use of the land is impossible. In this way, timber resources are being destroyed and tropical hardwoods have had to be protected, with restrictions on exporting them from the tropics. The amount of timber resource is declining in the tropics and causing concern.

> ℓ The candidate has given some reasons for the concern but drifts into consequences (soil erosion), rather than the timber resource theme expected. The reference to conservation measures is implicit rather than explicit. The approach is simplistic and lacks reference to the temperate areas of timber resource. This is a top Level 1 response, worth 3 marks.

■ ■ ■

Answer to question 1: Candidate B

(a) Non-renewable resources are those such as fossil fuels that have a finite life span at the current rate of extraction. They can only be replaced on a geological time scale. On the other hand, renewable resources, such as timber, can be used sustainably and thus replaced as they are exploited.

> This candidate ably sets out the distinction between the two types of resource, with examples. The definitions are explicit and succinct and show knowledge of the relevant concepts at a high level. This gains the full 4 marks.

(b) The life span of non-renewable resources can be extended in a number of ways. In the case of North Sea oil, the reserves were underestimated and far more oil has been discovered than originally thought. Technology has improved and more oil can be extracted, therefore extending the life of the individual fields. At the same time, more efficient use has been made of the oil products, as refining itself and car engines, for example, have become more efficient. Recycling of plastics has also reduced the need for the raw material.

> This is a full answer, incorporating a valid case study. The strategies are outlined and exemplified. This response gains all 4 marks.

(c) The continued exploitation of water resources is a cause for concern with regard to both the amounts available and the quality of the supply. Water is used for domestic, industrial and agricultural purposes in the LEDW. In addition, uses in the MEDW include recreation and tourism. The increase in population and variable rainfall in many areas of the LEDW causes an increase in demand for clean water at the same time as industrial demand increases. Pollution of water supplies by sewage and industrial effluent is increasing in areas such as Bangladesh, where people are affected by the spread of disease and chemical pollution from the Ganges. In some parts of the MEDW, the rate of water consumption is beginning to exceed supply. Dry summers and autumns in southeast England mean that water restrictions and conservation measures are necessary to enable demand to be met.

> This candidate outlines the causes of concern in the first sentence. This sets the scene clearly and the theme is exemplified with reference to the LEDW and the MEDW. The command word is heeded. This is clearly a good Level 3 response and is awarded the full 7 marks.

Managing cities: challenges and issues

Question 2

(a) Describe recent changes in the **CBD** that show decline in retailing. (4 marks)

(b) Explain why these changes have occurred. (4 marks)

(c) To what extent have strategies to reverse the decline in retailing in the **CBD** been successful? (7 marks)

■ ■ ■

Answer to question 2: Candidate A

(a) There has been a decline in retailing activity in recent years. Many shops have closed down because of competition from other shopping centres. Some areas on the fringes of the CBD have been abandoned, with the shops left empty or demolished.

> *e* There is some simple description of decline, though the candidate drifts into reasons, which are not required. The explanation cannot be credited in this section, but would have been acceptable as a response to part (b). The reference to the zone of assimilation is valid. There is so little relevant descriptive material that this response is awarded only 1 of the 4 marks available.

(b) The reasons for this decline are numerous. Modern retailers need more space and therefore need larger sites. They also want car-parking space, not easily found in CBDs because of the cost of land and access from main roads. New shopping centres in the suburbs are more attractive to shoppers as everything is under one roof. CBD sites were considered old and congested. Therefore, retailing has declined in the CBD.

> *e* This is a sound résumé of the reasons for the decline. However, the answer is not supported by examples. This range of points, straightforwardly expressed, gains 3 of the 4 marks available. More credit would have been gained if the candidate had made more of the relative attraction of competing centres.

(c) Many CBD retailing facilities have been rejuvenated. Local authorities have invested in renewing the local infrastructure by permitting wholesale redevelopment of city centres. In such cases, new shopping centres have been built next to, or on, existing high streets. Many shopping areas have been pedestrianised to allow hassle-free shopping. Traffic has been separated from retail areas and large car parks have been built on the outskirts of the retail area. There have also been many improvements in public transport. Small buildings have been demolished and local planners have permitted larger stores, owned by major chains, to be built. The centres have gained more specialised and higher-order stores.

🖊 Many of the strategies employed in centres are covered and some detail is provided. However, there is a lack of examples and no attempt to evaluate the strategies, as required by the question. Therefore, Level 3 cannot be attained. This is a good Level 2 response, worth 5 marks.

■ ■ ■

Answer to question 2: Candidate B

(a) Using Bromley, in Kent, as an example, in the CBD as a whole, many small, owner-run premises have been vacated. Shops selling, for instance, food, car spares, household furnishing, electrical goods and DIY materials have closed or moved out from the CBD. Shops on the fringes of the CBD (the zone of discard), such as small general shops, have been left derelict, as seen in London Road and Masons Hill.

🖊 This candidate demonstrates sound knowledge of the types, location and scale of recent decline and refers to theory. Relevant examples are included. This response is focused on the description requested, and gains full marks.

(b) The high cost of land in the CBD is an important reason for the decline in retailing. In Bromley, there was also a lack of large sites for shops to develop and of the necessary large-scale car parking. Traffic congestion was a frequent, time-consuming occurrence for both shoppers and shops. There was also increased competition from out-of-town shopping centres such as Lakeside Thurrock, which has thousands of free parking spaces and is just off the M25.

🖊 This is a well-focused response. The candidate covers the main reasons in outline and embeds them in the local example. This gains the full 4 marks.

(c) In Bromley, the local authority decided to compete with other shopping centres head on. A large site was made available by compulsory purchase to enable a developer to build a purpose-built centre, The Glades, adjacent and linked to the existing High Street. This ensured that large flagship stores (Marks and Spencer, Boots and Debenhams) would be included, as well as providing purpose-built stores for the large chains. Car parking for over 1300 cars was included, as well as a further 2500 spaces in other new car parks. The High Street was pedestrianised, thus improving the shopping ambience and allowing the two existing department stores (Allders and House of Fraser) to remain on their existing sites. Bromley successfully retained its status as a major Greater London shopping centre, with its large stores, specialist in both range and nature. However, the congestion from traffic has not been resolved and is still a feature at many times of day.

🖊 This is a good evaluation, well supported by the case study. A number of strategies are covered in detail. This is a clear Level 3 response, gaining full marks.

Recreation and tourism

Question 3

(a) **Distinguish between primary and secondary tourist resources.** (4 marks)

(b) **Outline the primary and secondary resources that have aided the growth of a named tourist resort.** (4 marks)

(c) **Evaluate the strategies used to manage tourism in a National Park in the UK.** (7 marks)

■ ■ ■

Answer to question 3: Candidate A

(a) Primary resources are those in the natural environment that people come to see. On the other hand, secondary resources are those in the human environment that people use.

e This is a simplistic distinction, offering little information in response to the question. It gains only 1 of the 4 marks available.

(b) In the tourist resort of Hastings in Sussex, the primary resources aiding the growth of the resort were the sea, the beach, the cliffs and the views along the coastline. The secondary resources included, originally, the castle, the Old Town and later hotels and guesthouses, resort amusements and the pier.

e This is a sound response, although there is some confusion regarding the castle and the Old Town, which are primary, not secondary, resources. However, the resources are applied correctly to Hastings. This response gains 3 of the 4 marks available.

(c) In the Peak District National Park, several strategies have been employed. As there are so many walkers, footpaths are reinforced to stop erosion and the widening of grass paths. So many people want to visit the area that limits have been placed on cars, forcing visitors to park and catch a minibus to where they want to go. Honeypots have been encouraged, so that people are concentrated into a few places where all the facilities are found. Public transport is encouraged, both bus and rail as appropriate.

e This is a sound response, covering a number of the most common strategies. However, the points are not fully developed so this response is in Level 2 and is awarded 4 marks.

■ ■ ■

Answer to question 3: Candidate B

(a) Primary resources are those in the natural environment that are of interest to people. They include scenery, climate and ecology, as well as historical and

heritage sites. Secondary resources, on the other hand, are purpose-built tourist facilities, such as accommodation, catering, entertainment, infrastructure and theme parks.

> ℮ This is a full response, with detail on both types of resource and examples at a general level. There is a clear attempt at the distinction. This response gains the full 4 marks.

(b) Disneyland Paris is based mainly on secondary resources. The only primary resource is the temperate climate (cool, wet winters and warm summers). The secondary resources include entertainment facilities in the park (plus Walt Disney Studios Park, next to the original park), 50 restaurants and ten hotels built as part of the resort. There are two other hotels a short distance away. A TGV/Eurostar station is on site, as well as good motorway links. There is also a shopping centre, outlet village and aquarium.

> ℮ This is a very good response. The resort is based on secondary resources, though primary are not omitted. There is good detail in the example and the respective roles of the resources in the growth of the resort are clear. This answer gains the full 4 marks.

(c) As there are so many visitors to the Peak District National Park (about 20 million people live within an hour's drive), management strategies have to be employed. The Pennine Way, a major long-distance footpath, runs through the park. In order to prevent and contain erosion of the path, it has been necessary to pave it. Facilities are concentrated into honeypots, such as Castleton. Hotels, restaurants, car parks, picnic areas and toilets are provided, as well as specialist tourist retail functions. Where traffic congestion is a concern, park-and-ride schemes are in operation (e.g. the Upper Derwent Valley, where over 3000 cars visit on bank holidays). In addition, road charging is being considered.

> ℮ This response contains similar material to that used by Candidate A. However, there is detailed support, making this a good Level 3 response, worth 7 marks.

Section B

Essays

Question 4

Food surpluses in the **MEDW** and food shortages in the **LEDW** are the natural
state of affairs. Discuss this statement.   (30 marks)

Question 5

Evaluate the success of initiatives to reduce deprivation in cities.   (30 marks)

Question 6

Tourism is the main stimulus for economic development in the **LEDW**.
Discuss this statement.   (30 marks)

✐ You must bear in mind that questions 4, 5 and 6 are synoptic in nature. In your response to
these questions you are required to show your knowledge and understanding of different
aspects of geography, the connections between these different aspects and, where relevant,
of human perspectives upon geographical themes and issues. The synoptic elements are
effectively considered by the inclusion of at least one of these three themes: physical–human
relationships, sustainability, environmental.

■ ■ ■

Answer to question 4: Candidate A

It is true to say that there are food surpluses in the MEDW and food shortages in the
LEDW, but the relationship is not straightforward and it is not certain whether the
relationship is temporary or permanent.

There are a number of reasons for food surpluses in the MEDW. In recent years,
trading blocs (e.g. the EU) have subsidised farming and farmers, encouraging them
to grow as much as possible to avoid food shortages. Farming has become more
efficient and output has increased. Subsidies are paid for each tonne of crops
harvested; guaranteed minimum prices are paid for other crops, regardless of the
output.

In the EU this resulted in surpluses of certain products, including butter, milk, beef,
cereals and wine. In addition, there were grants for using fertilisers, removing
hedgerows, clearing scrubland and so on, all of which contributed to the agricultural
surpluses.

This situation could not be kept up, as it was too expensive to the taxpayer. The
cost of storing the surpluses was several million pounds sterling every day. It was
decided in the late 1980s to tackle the surpluses. Milk output was reduced by about
10% and cereal farmers were paid £35 per hectare if the land was 'set-aside' and no
crops grown on it. Subsidies for beef and wine were also reduced in the 1990s.

It is clear that surpluses are no longer the norm in this part of the MEDW; they
have been reduced from the very high levels of the 1980s.

In the LEDW, the situation is reversed. Food shortages are common for a variety of reasons. Famine is widespread in many parts; in particular, the Sahel region of Africa has suffered drought to a greater or lesser extent over the last 20 years or so. At the same time, the population has been increasing rapidly, resulting in the well publicised famines. The farming systems use limited capital and technology and therefore yields are low.

The physical environment is often unhelpful, with high evapotranspiration rates, unreliable rains, flooding and droughts. The expansion of the deserts into the Sahel and the clearance of trees and shrubs, causing desertification, are also important factors. In many parts of Africa, there are food shortages.

On the other hand, in some parts of the LEDW, food supply is increasing and keeping up with the population increase. This is particularly so in areas where the green revolution has been employed. This involves using hybrids of, for example, rice, wheat and maize that produce much higher yields than the traditional crops.

In summary, it has been shown that there are indeed surpluses of food in the MEDW and shortages in the LEDW. However, it is clear that the surpluses are decreasing in the MEDW and there are areas in the LEDW without food shortages.

> *e* This candidate has demonstrated a good understanding of the main principles underpinning this topic. There is a clear essay format, with an introduction and a conclusion. Both elements in the LEDW and MEDW cases are covered and there is development of variants, enabling the candidate to evaluate and discuss the statement. The essay would have been improved by greater use and development of examples. The main limitation of the essay is that it does not demonstrate synopticity, which is reflected in the mark. This essay is a good Level 3 (13–18 marks) response.

■ ■ ■

Answer to question 4: Candidate B

Food surpluses are a recent phenomenon in the MEDW. However, all areas, including parts of the LEDW and the MEDW, have experienced, or are currently experiencing, food shortages.

To define a food shortage or surplus, reference must be made to population size. In much of the MEDW, populations are stable or slowly increasing; in some cases they are declining as population falls below replacement level. At the same time, until recently, food production has been increasing. Thus, food supply has risen at a greater rate than the population, resulting in surpluses.

The stabilisation of the population is demonstrated in the demographic transition model. Most countries in the MEDW have reached Stage 4 and may even have entered Stage 5 (decline), if this latter stage is more than a temporary fluctuation within Stage 4. As populations stabilise, the balance with food supply becomes increasingly relevant.

Governments have played a major role in increasing food supply in much of the MEDW, especially since 1950, in an effort to decrease dependency on overseas sources of food. Since the 1960s, the Common Agricultural Policy (CAP) has driven the increase in food production in Europe. As more countries have joined the European Union, the CAP has been important in encouraging farmers to increase output. A number of measures have been put in place.

Subsidies and grants were available for farmers to increase efficiency and intensify output. Farmers were encouraged to remove hedgerows, in order to increase field size and allow the more efficient use of machinery. In addition, increasing use was made of fertilisers, pesticides and herbicides. Grants were also available to increase the area of land under cultivation by reclaiming marginal land, whether by drainage or on slopes in marginal hill farm areas, as in the Lake District in the UK.

Prices paid to farmers for certain products, including beef, milk, cereals, wine and tobacco, were maintained by subsidies. Guaranteed prices were paid for these products and surplus stocks were purchased, regardless of the amounts produced. This led to the creation of wine and milk 'lakes' and wheat and butter 'mountains' and the expenditure of millions of euros on their storage or destruction. It is worth noting that not all products were subsidised in this way. For example, market gardening, and poultry and pig farming, operated in a more liberal market. Clearly, food surpluses were a feature of this part of the MEDW at this stage.

However, in recent years, the CAP has been amended in an effort to reduce the food surpluses. Quotas were first introduced to reduce the production of milk, beef, wool and lamb. Overall, milk production fell by over 20% in 10 years. Set-aside then followed, to reduce production of arable crops. Farmers taking 20% of their land out of cultivation received over £200 per hectare when keeping the land fallow. This figure was increased to £505 for the planting of conifers and £1375 for broadleaved woodland. Diversification into tourism, golf courses and nature trails was encouraged. Further cuts in production are envisaged as the new policy of paying farmers a subsidy per hectare regardless of the amount of crop or animal produced works its way through the farm economy. These subsidies are to be reduced over a number of years. In this way, farming is expected to become less intensive, aided by the increase in the area given over to organic farming.

As yet, food surpluses in the MEDW have not been totally eradicated. Indeed, it can be argued that surpluses are necessary to ensure food supplies in a time of potential world shortages, as the effects of global warming become more apparent, causing variations in the reliability of precipitation. Overall, the balance between food supply and consumption in the EU is yet to be achieved.

In many parts of the LEDW, food shortages are compounded by population growth. For example, the Sahel in Africa (situated between the Sahara Desert and the savanna grasslands) has summer rainfall that is variable both in amount and occurrence, permitting the growth of thorn scrub, with trees on dry watercourses. In the 1980s, the rains became very variable and failed in some years. This enabled the Sahara to 'expand' as the vegetation and crops died out. At the same time, wars in Ethiopia and the Horn of Africa caused disruption to agriculture and food supplies fell, leading to 'Band-Aid' and other fund-raising initiatives to provide emergency food aid for these areas. The political situation was stabilised in the 1990s and agricultural output

increased in Ethiopia and Somalia. The rains became less variable and the Saharan margins were shown to be fluctuating rather than expanding. However, despite the high death rate resulting from these conditions, the birth rate (over 50 per thousand) was one of the highest in the world. As conditions improved, the rise in population started to exceed the food supply again and, since 2000, the population–resource ratio has worsened and food shortages are now prevalent.

In contrast, food supplies have been increasing in many parts of the LEDW. The 'green revolution', involving the growth of hybrid seeds of maize (in Mexico) and rice (high-yielding IR8, in the Philippines and other areas of southeast Asia), greatly increased food supplies. The investment in fertilisers, drainage and improved cultivation techniques has meant that only the better-off can benefit, but in some areas food supplies have increased to more than compensate, thus contradicting the statement that food shortages are the natural state of affairs in the LEDW.

In recent years, many countries in the LEDW have seen a decline in the rate of population increase. This is due to the occurrence of the transition outlined in the demographic transition model and to increased death rates as a consequence of war, famine and disease. This is particularly the case in southern Africa, where AIDS is a potent factor in the increasing death rate. These factors are frequently interrelated, in that war and disease reduce the agricultural labour force and, consequently, farm output, as shown by the economic disruption in Zimbabwe as a result of the political impact of land reform.

The increasing cultivation in the LEDW of cash crops for Western markets and the dumping of MEDW surpluses on the world markets complicate the situation. For example, Kenya's farming output is increasingly dominated by crops such as roses, vegetables and coffee, produced for the UK market. This leads to a reduction in local food output and, potentially, to the need for imports. The export of surplus crops from the EU food mountains at subsidised prices, as well as the provision of food aid, results in local farmers in the LEDW being unable to sell their crops. Consequently, they stop farming, increasing the future food deficit even further.

In summary, it can be seen that the statement in the question is simplistic. There are undoubtedly areas of food surplus in the MEDW, but these surpluses are being tackled by farm reforms. The LEDW has areas of dire food shortage, but also areas with a more balanced population–resource ratio. The positions set out in the statement are extremes and certainly not 'the natural state of affairs', which is much more complicated.

   e This response has a clear essay structure, with an introduction and a conclusion. The question is fully addressed, with examples from different parts of the world. Reference is made to both the MEDW and the LEDW and this is maintained throughout the essay. Synopticity is demonstrated by links to the demographic transition model in Unit 2 and climatic conditions in the Sahel in Unit 1. Thus, the link between population and resources is well developed. Also, most of the other elements of Unit 5 are covered. This well-argued essay is lower Level 5 (25–30 marks).

Answer to question 5: Candidate A

In the MEDW, deprivation within cities has been the focus of policies and initiatives for many years. Deprivation is defined as when an individual's wellbeing falls below a reasonable level. In many inner-city areas, several socioeconomic factors may combine to indicate deprivation. This essay will place particular emphasis on the UK.

Deprivation is identified using social, economic and environmental criteria. Housing characteristics, income, employment and social class are all helpful in this identification. For example, poor-quality housing or overcrowding, low income or unemployment and low levels of education are identified in the census returns.

The type of area most affected by deprivation in the UK is the inner city, but additional deprived areas include the outer estates of social housing. Therefore, policies have been concentrated on these locations. Initially, after 1945, redevelopment of the oldest terraced housing was the main policy, along with the decanting of the population into New Towns in the surrounding countryside. This improved the standard of housing and, in many cases, employment was also available. The London New Towns included Crawley, Harlow, Stevenage and Bracknell, all situated about 25 miles from London with modern, purpose-built housing estates. Similar estates were constructed in London, for example in Peckham and Kidbrooke in south London.

However, this policy had certain limitations. In many cases, the housing was of poor quality, both in terms of design and endurance. This encouraged antisocial behaviour and crime. For this reason, the Ferrier estate, Kidbrooke, is about to be demolished. Many high-rise blocks of flats have been demolished because young families were often housed on the upper floors without space for children to play. In Hulme, Manchester, flats were converted into houses by removing the upper floors, and gardens were created.

It was realised that housing improvements would not by themselves solve the problems associated with deprivation. Multifaceted policies were introduced in the 1980s and this approach continues today. Whole areas have now been identified for improvement, involving housing, employment and, in the late 1990s, educational change. Development Corporations were established in the 1990s, one of the most famous being London Docklands. This large site of derelict former docks was handed over to the London Docklands Development Corporation (LDDC).

Over a period of 20 years from 1980, the infrastructure was improved (Docklands Light Railway (DLR), Jubilee Line extension, City Airport, Limehouse Link etc.), older housing was demolished, warehouses were converted into expensive apartments and new housing, both owner-occupied and social, was built. At Canary Wharf, large office blocks have been constructed, employing thousands, and the service needs of these workers are met by the hundreds of shops and restaurants in the complex.

The LDDC has been successful in transforming the economic landscape, but only the better qualified have benefited from the change as many jobs were moved from other areas of London (e.g. the City) and did not employ local people.

Since 1997, policies have broadened and education has been included in the multifaceted approach in an effort to raise educational standards and therefore improve the employment prospects of those living in inner London, among other areas.

Excellence in Cities and the establishment of specialist schools are two examples.

Similar problems are found in areas in the suburbs where large estates were built to house those displaced by redevelopment of inner areas. Kidbrooke was mentioned above; others include St Helier in southwest London and Downham and St Paul's Cray in southeast London. The housing has been upgraded in most cases. The Ferrier estate is about to be demolished and replaced with a mix of social, part-owned and owner-occupied housing. Along with the investment in education covered above, the intention is to tackle deprivation on a broad front in these areas.

Several policies have been in place over a number of years to try to reduce deprivation. The early policies were focused on housing and the environment; later ones included social and educational elements. The success of these recent policies is yet to be judged.

> 🖉 This is a reasonable, sound response. There is an essay format and the content is well expressed, with appropriate geographical terminology. The question is kept in mind throughout the essay. The points made are well supported by examples. However, the range is restricted, in that only a small number of policies from the MEDW are covered, and there is no synopticity. Therefore, this essay cannot achieve higher than Level 3 (13–18 marks), which it does with some ease.

■ ■ ■

Answer to question 5: Candidate B

Deprivation is defined as where the wellbeing of an individual or group of people is below a reasonable minimum. This definition has some flexibility and can be applied to cities in both the MEDW and the LEDW. In general, deprivation includes indicators from a range of socioeconomic criteria, including housing, education, health, employment or wealth and crime.

In the LEDW, initiatives are in response to the rapid growth of cities, as a result of natural increase (high birth rates) and in-migration from other parts of the country, or even further afield, or as a result of unequal economic development (as depicted in the core–periphery model). The scale of this increase in population results in large numbers of people (up to one-third of Mexico City's and 60% of Calcutta's population) showing characteristics of deprivation. This is seen in the development of shanties, in which poor-quality housing is set up illegally on any vacant land using any local materials to hand. The inhabitants of these shanties are poor and unemployed, or with low-paid employment or a job in the informal sector. Underemployment is common and people live at a subsistence level. Services for the shanties are few and far between. Drinking water is usually contaminated and there are no sewerage facilities. Electricity supplies are also limited. Education, if available, is at a basic level.

Initiatives have come from two sources: self-help by the people and government support. In South America, longer-established shanties are known as periferia. These have developed adequate standards because of their age and the input of the inhabitants. Authorities in São Paulo have provided some of the periferia with running water, drainage and electricity and, in a few cases, with roads and street lighting. Over time, these areas have continued to upgrade themselves, with shops and small industries being established at a later date. In Lusaka, Zambia, similar 'site and services' schemes have been established whereby the labour of the inhabitants is used to help build homes and the authorities provide water and drainage. Although these people remain poor, their lifestyle is improved and the level of deprivation stabilised or improved for many.

Richer countries in the LEDW have more grandiose initiatives. Clearance of shanties has occurred in Venezuela and Hong Kong. The replacement housing was in the form of high-rise apartments, close to the CBD, though in Hong Kong New Towns have also been built, close to the old border with China. As these are richer countries, the standards of living have risen with levels of economic development. Employment is more readily available as industry and commerce have become more important, especially in Hong Kong, which has moved towards take-off and may well have achieved it, according to the Rostow model. Educational standards are also higher, with all levels of education up to university offered in the area. Deprivation has not been eradicated in countries such as Hong Kong, but has been reduced for many.

In the MEDW, with particular reference to the UK, deprivation has been recognised in the inner cities and in many suburban estates of social housing. In these areas, the inhabitants live in poor-quality housing of different ages. Educational levels of achievement are low, resulting in either employment in low-paid jobs or unemployment. Crime levels are high, as are levels of illness and disease, the latter often as a result of poor diet. New migrants, both from within the country to the cities, and to the country, settle in these areas as housing costs are relatively low. These issues have been exacerbated as the better-off inhabitants move to the suburbs, thus concentrating the less well-off in these areas and confirming the effects of the push–pull (from the inner cities to the suburbs) model of migration.

Initiatives have long been in place to try to tackle deprivation in the UK. Until the 1970s, government policy was to tackle housing problems, rather than use a broader-based approach. Urban redevelopment, by means of comprehensive redevelopment of areas of nineteenth-century substandard housing, was the standard policy. The housing was replaced by new estates, often of social housing, either on the same site or in outer estates, both in the suburbs and in New Towns (or the equivalent). Examples of such development are the London New Towns (e.g. Crawley, Harlow, Stevenage) and the estates at Kidbrooke (Ferrier estate) and Peckham in London and Hulme in Manchester. These latter estates were built cheaply and often included high-rise blocks of flats. This approach destroyed the existing communities and failed to include strategies to improve education and employment opportunities. The improvements in housing over the older housing proved illusory, as problems of construction and design soon became apparent and crime levels rose as the built environment encouraged anti-social behaviour.

A policy of urban renewal was employed for nineteenth-century housing that was of better quality. Private owners in General Improvement Areas (GIA) usually carried this out, as in Islington, which in this case became part of the process of

gentrification. Grants were provided for the refurbishment. Many large houses were subdivided into flats. All housing was provided with bathrooms, an indoor lavatory and other facilities now taken for granted by most people.

Initiatives changed in the 1980s. Government bodies led regeneration projects and local authorities lost their powers in favour of housing associations. Former council estates were passed to housing associations to become Housing Action Trusts. These involved tenants in improving and refurbishing whole estates, as in Hulme, Manchester. High-rise blocks were demolished and blocks of maisonettes were converted into houses. At the same time, policy shifted to a broader approach involving both housing and economic regeneration.

The London Docklands Development Corporation (LDDC) took over responsibility for the large area of derelict docks and their environs. Housing was improved in a number of ways. Old warehouses were converted into luxury apartments, thus broadening the social mix of the area, but not actually integrating it. Social housing was provided, as well as low-cost accommodation, thus enabling local people to remain. Economic regeneration was kick-started by land clearance and the provision of transport infrastructure (Jubilee Line extension, Docklands Light Railway, City Airport, Limehouse Link road and so on). The private sector was then able to develop both housing and commercial projects, with Canary Wharf as the beacon. The employment generated by the large office developments at Canary Wharf (now over 20 000 people employed), and the subsequent provision of over 200 shops and restaurants, have given a huge economic boost to the area and indeed to London as a whole.

However, local people missed out when their jobs were lost as part of the economic change. The new jobs were for the highly skilled and most were relocated from other parts of London. The strand of policy starting in the 1990s involved education and training for the first time, the point being that a better-educated and trained workforce would help to reduce and eventually remove deprivation. The 'Excellence in Cities' initiative and 'City Academies' have already helped to improve educational standards; policies to ensure that adults attain at least a Level 2 qualification are in place. Educational Maintenance Allowances have been piloted in the inner-city areas; these offer a payment of £30 per week in London for students aged 16–18 with good attendance and progress. The success of the recent policies is yet to be fully evaluated, but the nature of the schemes, now focused on deprivation, offers a better chance of overall success.

In summary, deprivation is found in cities throughout the world. Initiatives have been applied in both the LEDW and the MEDW. In the LEDW, they rely on economic growth and change to make an impact as government funds are limited, but the rate of population increase means that initiatives are under pressure to start with. In the MEDW, initiatives have been in place for a longer time and investment is greater. There has been some success, but broad, multifaceted policies are of recent origin and success in the reduction of deprivation depends on economic growth and the willingness of people to take up the skills and training opportunities.

📝 This is a broad-ranging essay. There is a clear essay format and terms are defined at the start. Both the LEDW and the MEDW contexts are addressed and, in each case, there is a wide range of examples. The command words are kept to the fore and are considered in a focused manner. Evaluation occurs consistently throughout. There are a number of references to synoptic material, particularly to Unit 2 (all three elements). This response attains upper Level 5 (25–30 marks).

■ ■ ■

Answer to question 6: Candidate A

Tourism is an important factor in economic development in the LEDW. It is only in the last few years that tourism has become increasingly important in the LEDW; previously, the focus was in the MEDW from where most tourists originate. Tourism in the LEDW was originally of two types. The rich went to the most exotic locations, such as the Seychelles and Mauritius, away from the masses, while the young backpacked to more accessible, but exotic, locations, such as India, Nepal or Goa.

Currently, much of the LEDW is accessible to tourists. Its attraction has always been the unspoilt primary resources, such as wildlife, scenery and climate. However, in recent years, virtually all countries in the LEDW have tried to attract tourists by building secondary resources, such as hotels, airports and resorts. This interest in tourism is fuelled by the potential economic gains the country hopes to make from tourists visiting their country. For many countries, tourism is considered to be the stimulus for economic growth.

The money from tourism is of benefit to a country. It is much-needed foreign exchange. The money spent acts as a multiplier, passing through the economy and expanding the wealth of the country as it does so. Local people are employed in the hotels, airports and in servicing the tourist attractions. Local farming may be stimulated by the need for food for the guests in the hotels. However, the employment opportunities are low level, the management and other posts usually being held by foreign nationals. Thus, the local labour force remains unskilled and those skills they learn from the employment are not transferable to the rest of the economy.

The profits gained from the tourist industry are usually sent abroad, as the infrastructure, such as hotels and the attractions, are sold as packages by multinational companies. These are foreign-owned and therefore will repatriate profits. On the other hand, it is because they are multinational concerns that they have the capital to invest in the tourist infrastructure in the first place. These companies may improve the infrastructure of the country, either directly by road building or indirectly by causing governments to provide the infrastructure for the tourists. Egypt earns $3 billion each year from tourism, a significant contribution to the balance of payments. A large proportion of the $2.2 billion inward investment is to provide infrastructure for the tourist sector of the economy.

The main economic drawback of a reliance on tourism is that fashions can change and tourists may no longer wish to visit the attractions of the country. As tourist activity is such a large proportion of the economy of an LEDC, any such change has a deleterious impact. Bali suffered greatly after the bombing of the nightclub by terrorists; few tourists now visit Bali, over a year after the event. The local economy

has been devastated, with high levels of unemployment, as a downward multiplier has set in.

In east Africa, the authorities realised that the traditional tourist activity of big game hunting was no longer viable and changed to safaris by truck, observing the wildlife at close quarters. The difficulties caused by erosion by the vehicles have been reduced by offering balloon trips to view the wildlife. This reinforces the need to update facilities to keep tourists coming. Better secondary resources have been constructed as the tourist market in Kenya has expanded to include both inland safaris and coastal resort facilities.

Other types of tourism, other than mass tourism, in the LEDW include ecotourism, also referred to as sustainable tourism. This has as little impact as possible on the local environment. In Costa Rica, in Central America, tourism is strongly influenced by the government. The main attractions include volcanoes, rainforest, cloud forest and high plateaux (each with its characteristic wildlife habitats) in National Parks and conservation areas. In addition, fishing, surfing and wind surfing are available on the coast. Development of tourist infrastructure is deliberately limited to respect the environment and the local culture. Hotels are small, usually less than 100 rooms, and have basic amenities to reduce the impact on the environment. Many hotels are owned and run by local people. Tourism generates about 9% of Costa Rica's GDP, generating an income of $1 billion and employing 75 000 people. Tourism is important to the economy of Costa Rica but, at this level of contribution to the economy, the country is not reliant on it.

From these examples, it can be seen that tourism plays an important part in the economic development of countries in the LEDW. For many, it is the main stimulus and provides numerous benefits. It also has economic disadvantages, as shown above. Problems can be caused if the country is over-reliant on the income generated and the tourists subsequently decide to go elsewhere. By itself, tourism cannot, and should not, be the main stimulus for the economic development of a country in the LEDW.

> ℮ This response shows limited understanding. There is a clear essay format and competent use of appropriate terminology. Cases are used to a variable extent, and are valid. The link between economic development and tourism is made, but is not developed to show other strategies that could have an impact on economic development. There is insufficient evaluation, the need for which is implicit in the question. Also, there is no clear evidence of synopticity. Therefore, this is an upper Level 3 (13–18 marks) response.

■ ■ ■

Answer to question 6: Candidate B

Tourism in the LEDW is certainly used as a stimulus for economic development. However, it is only one of many stimuli that could be employed, either separately or in combination, depending on the individual economic, social and environmental conditions in the country concerned.

Examples of tourism as the main stimulus for economic development can be identified in many parts of the LEDW. The Seychelles and Mauritius are tropical islands in the Indian Ocean. As small islands, there are few alternatives to stimulate economic development. Sugar cane and palm products are produced, but agriculture is limited in scale. The primary resources of tropical climate, sandy beaches, coral atolls and tropical sea are the main attractions to tourists. The secondary resources constructed to meet the tourist demand include the airport, hotels and sporting facilities, both land and sea oriented. It is the remoteness and exclusivity of these islands that make them attractive to the visitors, who can stay in a range of hotels, from large (200 rooms) to small and intimate (20 rooms). The income from tourism is very important to the Seychelles and Mauritius as a major source of foreign exchange to aid the balance of payments. In addition, it acts as a multiplier, passing through the economy and increasing the wealth of the local population by creating employment in tourist-related activities. These jobs occur both directly in the hotels and in associated small businesses, concerned with water sports or handmade crafts.

As might be expected, the economic benefits are offset to some extent by disad-vantages. For instance, the hotels and major tourist facilities are owned by, and the exclusive packages sold by, foreign multinational companies (e.g. Abercrombie and Kent). Therefore, the profits are exported to the country of origin of these companies. In addition, foreign nationals usually fill the most senior posts and the local labour force does not have the opportunity to gain higher management skills for the benefit of the wider economy.

In Costa Rica, the government has approached tourism differently, that is, ecotourism. This is a sustainable approach and does not rely on mass tourism as so many other countries in the LEDW do. Hotels are small and basic, but exclusivity is maintained by the small numbers of tourists who come to see the scenery. Today, tourism contributes about $1 billion to the economy, which is about 10% of GDP. Therefore, economic development is not reliant on this activity.

Some countries in the LEDW have other resources that can be used to stimulate economic growth. For example, in the 1980s Gambia was reliant on the export of groundnuts (90% of GDP) but has now diversified into tourism and has a more balanced economy. However, the issues outlined above are still applicable. As a major oil producer, Venezuela is a member of OPEC. The income from oil has aided the diversification of the economy. Growth theory was used to concentrate economic development into a small number of growth poles, near to and including the capital Caracas, allowing the processes outlined in the core–periphery model to operate. Industrialisation was concentrated into these poles. Venezuela does not have a large tourist sector and, it could be argued, has been over-dependent on oil at the expense of other sectors of the economy that are relatively less well developed.

Countries in the LEDW tend to have economies with a large primary sector, being dependent on agriculture, forestry, mining or quarrying, and fishing. Some countries possess mineral resources that can be exported; others have tried to expand secondary industry, based on the raw materials available to them. Success has been variable. In countries such as Singapore and Hong Kong, imported raw materials, a skilled, well-

educated labour force and a favourable investment climate have enabled the economy to follow the development stage model from primary, via secondary, into a thriving tertiary sector. In both these cases, this does include tourism, but the economies of these small countries are not totally dependent on tourist income.

India has diversified away from a large primary sector (agriculture and mining) by means of rapid growth of the manufacturing industry over the last 20 years or so. Its tertiary sector is also expanding rapidly, as demonstrated by the growth in the call-centre services and routine data-processing functions for companies in the MEDW. Nonetheless, tourism is an important strand within the tertiary sector, as represented by the Taj Mahal and the coastal resort of Goa. The primary tourist resources are the attraction and these cannot be accessed by tourists without the necessary secondary tourist infrastructure being in place. The demand tends to come from the MEDW, so is driven by the wealth and free time of people in these countries, which is recognised by the tourist operators and translated into visitors to the countries in the LEDW.

The model of tourist development proposed by Butler is relevant in considering the importance of tourism in economic development.

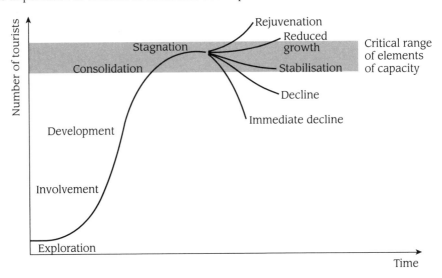

Most LEDCs are in the stages of involvement, development and consolidation. For any country involved in tourism, a change in fashion or another negative event could lead to decline, causing a severe downward multiplier, via unemployment. For one dependent on tourism as the stimulus for economic development, the effects would be deleterious to the local and national economy. The impact on tourism in Bali of the recent terrorist bomb has been to virtually destroy the sector, as most MEDCs still advise against travelling to Indonesia. On the other hand, the bombs in Istanbul have had less impact on tourism in Turkey because the advice against travelling was lifted soon after the event and the main tourist areas of Turkey were not involved. Turkey also has a broad-based economy, not totally reliant on tourism, although the sector is important.

The outbreak of SARS had a similar effect. The Far East, particularly Hong Kong, was affected as virtually all tourist travel ceased during the epidemic. Tourist numbers have not yet returned to pre-epidemic levels.

In summary, the role played by tourism in economic development varies from country to country in the LEDW. It is the main stimulus in some countries, particularly those that are small or which have limited alternative resources that could be used to stimulate economic development. This can result in over-dependence and lead to the risk of rapid dislocation when the tourist numbers decline. In larger countries, the stimuli for economic development are frequently more varied, thus providing a broader base to the economy. In this case, tourism is not the main stimulus for economic development, but one of a number of such stimuli.

ⓔ This is a very good response. The essay style is well developed, with a focused introduction and conclusion. The candidate consistently refers to the theme and the command words are followed. The evaluation implicit in the question wording is present throughout. A range of appropriate cases is used from a variety of locations in the LEDW and there is reference to relevant theory. Synopticity is evident, particularly in the use of material from Unit 2. Therefore, this is an upper Level 5 response (25–30 marks).